DESCENT INTO CONFLICT, 1945

A Doctor's War

DESCENT INTO CONFLICT, 1945

A Doctor's War

David H. Clark

The Book Guild Ltd
Sussex, England

The Book Guild Ltd.
25 High Street,
Lewes, Sussex

First published 1995
© David H. Clark 1995

Set in Times
Typsetting by Raven Typesetter, Chester, Cheshire

Printed in Great Britain by
Antony Rowe Ltd.
Chippenham, Wiltshire

A catalogue record for this book
is available from the British Library

ISBN 1 85776 006 9

CONTENTS

ACKNOWLEDGEMENTS

After telling my war stories for many years I decided, when I reached seventy years of age, to write them down for the interest of my children, stepchildren and grandchildren. This made a small book so I gave a few copies to friends. The response was so positive that I was persuaded to prepare it for publication. When I tried to put the story together I was helped by a few records, notably the letters I had sent home from war service which were kept by my mother and by Mary Rose Clark. I also had a diary of my Sumatran experience; I mislaid this in a transit camp in Burma in 1946, but it was returned to me in 1949 by Dr Ronald Emond to whom I am also grateful. In the task of producing a readable tale in the 1990s I am deeply grateful to Julie Aston who typed draft after draft and endured my endless corrections and vacillations. My thanks also go to my editors, Pip Hardy and Chantal Porter of The Book Guild who finally pulled the book together.

For Margaret

PREFACE

This is an account of what happened to me in the tumultuous and exciting year 1945 – I am writing it down now, in the 1990s, in my seventies, before the memory of those exciting days completely fades. I am writing it partly for my children and grandchildren so that they may know something of what made their grandfather how he is, but mostly to make sense of it for myself. For many years I have had a busy but quiet professional life, far from violence and danger. It seems strange that once I jumped out of aeroplanes, endured battle and fear, saw death, wounding and devastation and was taken half way round a world full of disintegration, revolution and violence. But it did happen, many years ago, and this is the tale. To tell it fully I must tell how I got there in the first place.

EARLY DAYS

My father, Alfred Joseph Clark, was a medical scientist of some standing. Born in 1885 into a prosperous Somerset Quaker family, he was a brilliant student who studied medicine in Cambridge and London before settling to the new science of pharmacology. He spent time in Germany as a student at Marburg and loved the Germans, their language, their science and their culture, all his life. In World War 1, he felt it his duty to serve in the army. He broke with his family, their pacifist tradition and the Society of Friends, enlisted and spent three years on the western front as a medical officer ending as a major with a Military Cross. These years left a permanent mark on him and he often referred to them.

After the war he was briefly in South Africa where he met and married my mother, Beatrice Hazell, a schoolteacher with vigorous opinions and tireless tongue. They had in common a love of mountaineering, passionate anticlericalism and agnosticism, vigorous questioning intellectualism, an aversion to all forms of music and a devotion to the moral code of duty and priorities preached by Rudyard Kipling. I was born in 1920, their first child, in London where father had moved to a professorship. When I was six he moved to another professorship at Edinburgh. I grew up in that cold, grey, windy city and had my schooling as a day boy at George Watson's College grammar school, an obdurate, garrulous English boy amongst hostile Scots.

I think I was originally a rather soft gentle child. Certainly I was known as 'Bubbles' at the age of five. Under pressure of my mother's spartan creed and the pressures of school, I worked hard to try to become a tough boy. I played rugger, cricket, swimming and athletics – all incompetently, for I was fat, clumsy and ill co-

3

ordinated, though vigorous, impetuous and large. I walked the hills of southern Scotland, went camping, youth hostelling and trout fishing.

I was good at my school work and often won prizes, which delighted my father and mother, both of whom had been outstanding students who paid their way through their universities by scholarships and bursaries. They encouraged me in competitive study. My best subjects were English and history; I loved tales of old romance and enjoyed trying to tell again the stories of heroes of old. I devoured Scott and Robert Louis Stevenson and knew of all the deeds of Wallace and Bruce. My father noted my interest in biology – in egg collecting, fishing and keeping pet animals – and decided that I would be a biologist like him.

At school we had to learn a foreign language and were offered the choice of French or German. My father remarked that French was no use to a scientist, whereas German was essential. So I began to study German and in due course was sent to Germany during holidays to improve my command of the language.

The 1930s were the years of my adolescence and my awakening to social issues. We lived a comfortable life in a middle-class suburb of Edinburgh, Morningside. Although we had no motor car, my mother had two living-in servants to do the housework. I could not, however, be unaware of social inequality and the suffering of the poor. Edinburgh stood in the middle of a coal mining area and in the 1930s unemployment was widespread. Our maids came from villages where every man was out of work and had been for years. On my way to school I passed the 'Booroo' – the labour exchange where on Thursdays the streets filled with lean-faced men in caps and mufflers waiting to draw the dole. The government was in England, Conservative and complacent. I burned with youthful indignation, read H. G. Wells and began to call myself a socialist.

I read widely, omnivorously and indiscriminately. One wet summer holidays I read my way through the entire Waverley novels! I read Conan Doyle, Dumas, Buchan and my parents' favourites, Kipling, Hardy and George Eliot. But the writer who truly fired my imagination was H. G. Wells. I read the *Outline of History* and the *Science of Life;* I read the science fiction and all the short stories; I read *Kipps, Tono Bungay, Mr Polly,* but most of all I read the books which Wells was publishing regularly in the 1930s – polemics that attacked the stupidity of the Conservatives, of the traditionalists, and of the religious, books which proclaimed that all the world needed for universal peace and brotherhood was honesty, clear thinking, science and socialism (all of which I felt were mine). He made it clear that war was an out of date anachronism; that no one in their senses wanted war; that it was only ignorance, greed and religious superstition that produced war.

In 1936, when I was in my last year at school and committed to science and a career in medicine, I went to Germany again to improve my German. An exchange was arranged through an official agency. I was sent to a family in south Germany; a young German came to our home.

To my surprise I found out that they were deeply committed National Socialists. The youth, Karl, distressed my father by spouting a version of World War I history that he did not recognise. In Calw I found myself in a home full of enthusiasm for the new order. I was shown towns clean, happy and industrious – no unemployed, no decaying industry, no sullen resentment as in Scotland and I was very impressed. They said to me 'Ah, David, you are a socialist, but we are national socialists – and that is much better'.

They saw in me a potential recruit and arranged for me to spend two weeks at a Hiltler Youth camp. It was a well run camp in delightful country beside the Bodensee. The lads were friendly and cheerful; we played games, went for walks and went marching.

At first I liked it – but then I gradually became more and more uneasy. I realised that these lads were happily and busily preparing for war – a war of conquest of Europe. We sang as we marched – jolly songs, with lively tunes but terrifying refrains such as: *'Denn heute gehört uns Deutschland, und morgen die ganze Welt'.* ('For today Germany belongs to us and tomorrow the whole world.') In the evenings we were given lectures on race history, on the German colonies and how they had been stolen, on race knowledge and on the inferiority of the French who mixed their blood with negroes, and on the evil of the Jews who – I was told – had taken over my country and the United States. Everyone there knew that Roosevelt and Churchill were Jews.

I was appalled. I held my tongue (with difficulty) and returned home. I told my parents that the Germans were aiming to conquer the world and that war would come soon. I begged to be allowed to join the School Officer Training Corps, to be prepared. My parents believed me (they had met young Karl) but most people did not. It was Olympic year 1936 and the Germans had been very gracious hosts, assuring English visitors that they wished no conflict with us as we were fellow Aryans (though misled).

Then Britain was swept by the abdication crisis. To me, as a youth of 16, it seemed another example of the stuffy religious old men (Baldwin and the Archbishop of Canterbury) destroying a charming young man in love and sending the hope of the country away.

During those years there must have been discussions about my future – though of course in the custom of those days, I heard about it afterward. I was academically successful and interested in biology; my father concluded that I should become a research scientist, like himself – he could think of no better life for anyone. I should, therefore, go to Cambridge, to his old college, Kings, and study medicine.

So the programme was set. In 1937, aged 17, I passed the Scottish Higher School Leaving Certificate. I could have stayed on in the senior form at school, but my father thought it better for me to start straight in at Edinburgh University working through the premedical sciences and the anatomy dissections. I was sent to live in the 'University Settlement' where we gave voluntary service running boys' clubs for the very poor in a working class housing estate, and my socialist commitment deepened.

In the summer of 1938 I went to Cape Town in South Africa to visit my grandmother and aunt. I was delighted by the beautiful land and the friendly hospitable people – and appalled by the racist assumptions of the whole society and the hostility between the English and the Afrikaaners. During the three week boat journey home the Munich crisis erupted and war seemed inevitable. Then tension subsided and in October 1938 I went to Cambridge, to King's College to start my proper medical studies.

Although looking back from my seventies I may seem critical of what two earnest young people pushed into the head of a malleable little boy in the 1920s and 1930s, I had a most fortunate, and happy childhood. My mother and father showered affection upon me – for I seemed to be developing all those characteristics which they most prized in themselves and most hoped for in their offspring. I was cosseted in regard and reward (not undemanding or uncritical) but nevertheless heartening and warming. Whenever I did well at school (frequently) or at sports (rarely), I was praised and rewarded liberally with frequent homilies explaining why they rewarded what they did. I believed I had the best of parents – kind, just and rewarding.

Looking back, I feel I had three messages from my parents – be intelligent, be scientific, be brave. Being intelligent meant knowing a lot of facts and talking about them; it also meant succeeding in examinations. Being scientific meant being sceptical and anticlerical, only interested in proven facts and immediately suspicious of myths, fairy tales and established religion. Being brave meant being able to walk long distances, to climb mountains, to take part in painful sports without complaint.

MEDICAL STUDENT

I arrived at Cambridge in October 1938 filled with both confidence and uncertainty – like any other adolescent. I knew I was going to my father's college and I believed I was going to repeat his activities and successes. I was going to row, I was going to study medical science, I was going to win distinction, I was going to become a doctor and later a distinguished medical scientist. Everyone told me so. On the other hand, I felt myself to be an uncouth provincial amongst the assured products of the English public schools, suave and self confident.

Although I was tall – six foot – and heavy – 12 stone – I knew I was incompetent at most sports and games. Further, I felt ill at ease amongst my contemporaries. I had not liked the Scots amongst whom I grew up and I had been unpopular at school. But I found I disliked the arrogant undergraduates with their assumption of innate superiority and also the cringing fawning townfolk of Cambridge who it appeared would swallow any indignity provided they were adequately paid.

And there was the coming war. Although I was glad, as everyone was, that the Munich settlement had averted war in September 1938, I knew it was only a postponement. I knew that the Nazis were set on world conquest and I knew that we would have to fight them. At Cambridge I found many others who accepted that fact, with the bitter certainty of youth. We felt that the country was governed by fatuous nincompoops – McDonald, Baldwin and Chamberlain – who were so frightened of war that they were pretending that it would not come; further, they were not doing enough to prepare for it.

I applied myself to my necessary tasks. I joined the King's

8

College rowing club and rowed every afternoon on the river. I joined the Cambridge University Officers Training Corps and trained as an artillery officer, taking and passing the various certificates. I attended lectures, classes, laboratories and supervision.

In the Spring of 1939 Hitler invaded Czechoslovakia and even Neville Chamberlain realised his 'peace in our time' was a vain hope. I remember how we said goodbye in Cambridge that Easter vacation, believing that the war might start before we got back. We saw ourselves a 'doomed generation'. We were just the right age – 19 – for army service and we knew that nearly all those who were 19 in 1914 were dead by 1918. At King's we heard often about Rupert Brooke – the poet who had written 'If I should die, think only this of me'; he had been a brilliant student and young don at King's before going off to die, and many senior members of the college spoke of him with emotion and affection.

It was, I think, about that time that I became convinced that I too was doomed to die young and never grow old. I remember cherishing Alan Seeger's poem:

> I have a rendezvous with Death
> At some disputed barricade,
> When Spring comes back with rustling shade
> And apple blossoms fill the air . . .
> I shall not fail that rendezvous

The summer term of exams passed. Since war seemed imminent I gave up plans to take a holiday on the continent and set out to cycle round Britain. I said to my parents, 'Since I am about to die for England, I think I had better see what it looks like!' I cycled from Cambridge up the east coast to Edinburgh, from Edinburgh down the west coast to Somerset, and back across southern England to Cambridge – 1,000 miles in three weeks – a memorable trip. I saw squalor worse than I had ever imagined, in Lancashire, in Wigan and in Preston and I saw beautiful countryside – Cheshire, Herefordshire, Somerset and Salisbury Plain – that entranced me. It was so much richer, warmer and more beautiful than the bare bleak hills of Scotland.

I was back in Edinburgh by mid August 1939 when the

9

inevitable war came. The tension escalated. We listened to wireless bulletins, we bought black-out material, we oiled ancient shutters, we began to dig an air raid shelter in the back garden and Father instructed us on how to fill sand bags and revet a trench.

On Sunday 3 September 1939 we went down to his laboratory in the New Quad of Edinburgh University to fill and pile sand bags to protect vital points. I remember it clearly, a beautiful bright sunny morning. At midday we stopped our work and gathered outside the sitting room window of Forge, the head porter, to listen to his wireless set. At noon we heard the sad defeated voice of Chamberlain telling us that 'a state of war now exists between this country and Germany'. Almost as soon as he had finished, the air raid sirens went off! It was the predicted immediate devastation! But after a short time the all-clear went and we learned that it had been a false alarm.

Then came the strange period of the 'phoney war' which lasted all through the bitter cold winter of 1939–40. At first there was brisk bustle – the army and navy reservists were called up, the grand fleet moved to Orkney and there were uniforms everywhere. But then things settled down. As a trained artillery officer, I expected to be called up right away. Rather to my surprise I was told to get on with my medical training. I was told that I would be far more useful as a doctor in a few years' time than as an artillery officer now!

I went back to Cambridge and got on with taking my exams. My father was recalled to the army as a colonel in the Royal Army Medical Corps, to advise on poison gas, which everyone expected would be used.

By this time I was rather more at ease in Cambridge and I moved into rooms in college with two other medical students, Bob Turner and Irvine Smith. We had a group of friends and a lively social life. I had given up rowing (having done badly at that, too) and was now learning judo. My interest in politics had grown greatly. I studied the classic writings and debated endlessly. I saw the great films such as *The Battleship Potemkin* and heard noted socialist speakers who came to Cambridge, such as Cripps, Dalton, Attlee and Gallagher.

I was committed to socialism and attracted to communism; the most active, committed and effective socialists were all members of 'The Party'. However, when the Soviet Union attacked Finland, their casuistry in defending the indefensible turned me against them, as did their devious (and successful) manipulations to gain control of the funds of the University Socialist Society. I labelled myself a 'Democratic Socialist'.

All through the winter of 1939–40 we felt confident – though puzzled. Received Opinion was clear; the Germans could not win; the French were secure behind the Maginot line; the British empire was secure behind the British navy and was arming itself and would eventually annihilate the Germans; there was no cause for worry, or even for exertion. The navy had swept the seas clear and defeated the submarines – look how they had defeated the *Graf Spee* in the Battle of the River Plate! Then came the extraordinary spring and summer of 1940. The Germans invaded and conquered Denmark and Norway. Then they swept over Holland and Belgium and on to the Channel. All certainties were wiped away. Parliament threw Chamberlain out of office and Churchill became Prime Minister. Soon he began to address us on the radio. His wonderful rhetoric stirred me deeply. For the first time in my life, I felt some confidence in the government of the country and our leadership.

It was a lovely summer of hot sunny days. In Cambridge we were sitting our tripos examinations and were anxious and busy. But between exams we swam, punted and entertained our girlfriends. Yet, not far away, the world was changing. The Germans captured the Channel ports. Some evenings we could hear a distant thunder-like rumbling in the east, the guns around Dunkirk. Our examinations seemed fatuous and irrelevant. The May balls were cancelled and we were sent home as soon as our exams finished.

I came home to Edinburgh to find my father thinner and shaken. He had been called to Belgium when the Germans tanks broke through, had been through the chaos of the retreat, had been used as an ordinary doctor for a week and then shipped out through Dunkirk. 'This is a young man's war,' he said sadly. At this time I suffered my own personal defeat. The tripos results came through; I had not got a First – as my father had expected. I

11

had already realised that I was not as clever as the best of my fellow students at Cambridge, but now he had to face it too. He concluded that I could never make a scientific career like his. Though he never reproached me, his disappointment was unmistakable.

In July 1940 I found myself idle and useless in Edinburgh in glorious summer weather while the world was falling apart. I went off on a walking trip round my favourite youth hostels, but the news that Paris had fallen to the Germans drove me home. I had to find something useful to do, some contribution to make. My father found me a place as a surgical dresser on the wards of the Royal Infirmary and later a job harvesting. I sharpened the World War I bayonets that we had used for weeding the lawns and awaited the invasion. It never came.

All through the summer we heard of the air battles over southern England and the bombing of London – and fretted as to what we could do. I did not want to go back to the theoretical life of Cambridge; I wanted to get on with becoming a doctor and being useful in the great struggle. I transferred my studies to Edinburgh and joined the third (clinical) year there.

By the autumn of 1940 I was back in the familiar Scots lecture theatres of the medical school and on the wards of the Royal Infirmary – amongst a new group of fellow students. It was a hard life – as the life of medical students always is; many lectures, many exams, long hours on the wards and in the operating theatres. I lived at home and cycled in to classes every day. The war became harsher and ever drearier. Food became short and I stayed my hunger with bread and potatoes.

But much of the traditional life of medical students also went on; parties, drinking, dances, girlfriends, long intense serious discussions of politics and ethics, philosophy and religion. I made two good friends – also outsiders amongst the Scots like myself – Gus Born, a refugee from Germany and Dan Cunningham, an Oxford transfer – but also found a place amongst the medical students, joining societies, writing for the 'Student' magazine. I took up cross country running (again I was not much good), taught judo and spent my holidays felling trees for the Forestry Commission.

In the summer of 1941 I suffered another personal defeat.

Hearing how the medical schools of England were disrupted and dispersed by the bombing of London in 1940, the Rockefeller Foundation offered places in American medical schools for selected British medical students. It was decided to select them like the Rhodes scholars, to choose men who were outstanding in their studies, in sport and in student affairs. Nominees were called for from every British medical school. I was one of two from Edinburgh. I was proud and my father pleased. An eminent committee of 30 professors met in London to interview the candidates. I went down and spoke confidently of my knowledge of American life and letters; I thought I had done well. I was rejected. A stolid classmate was sent to America instead of me. I was shattered and my father dismayed. It was years later that I heard that I 'had talked myself out of a place' by my brash bumptiousness.

In 1941, home life changed dramatically. My mother, tuberculous since 1932, had developed advanced lung tuberculosis in 1940 and in 1941 was gravely, possibly mortally, ill. Then my father collapsed suddenly with intestinal obstruction in July 1941 and died three days later.

At 21, I found myself head of the family. The other children were younger, Gwen 18, Ralph 15 and June 12; my mother was grievously ill. I was made an executor of father's will and laden with business. Many decisions had to be made and I had to implement most of them. We were not poor, but it was difficult to manage and uncles, though helpful, were engaged in their own war work.

After my father's death I grew closer to my mother. I was her first born and her favourite, and during my school days she had committed much time to my school work, correcting my Latin, overseeing my reading of English literature and coaching me for elocution contests, but as I grew into adolescence she had given more attention to my sisters and brother. She had encouraged me to take holidays on my own and sent me to Germany in 1935 and 1936, Canada in 1937 and South Africa in 1938, partly because she believed it was good for the young to be sent away from home, 'to have their raw edges rubbed off'. She constantly expounded spartan creeds of self reliance, hardihood and independence, usually backing them with quotations from Kipling.

In my early childhood she was very active and vigorous, play-ing mixed hockey and going on mountaineering trips to the Alps, but when I was twelve she developed pulmonary tuberculosis, in those days a progressive incurable disease. She spent time in sanatoriums and had a thoracoplasty in 1933; she made a fair recovery but was never strong again and spent much of her time in an 'open air' hut in the garden – a common prescription for the tuberculous in those days. In 1940 she developed pneumonia which reactivated her tuberculosis. By the summer of 1941 she was grievously ill, lying in bed all day, coughing blood, with her temperature swinging over 104°F every afternoon.

Then came my father's sudden unexpected death in July 1941; she realised that it was her duty to rear the four children alone. Now I had to work with her all the time. I was her only confidant and we spent many long hours, partly in business and partly in talk, often about the war and its strategies (which she followed avidly from her bed) but often about life and people that she had known. I shared nearly everything with her, though I learned to avoid expounding my deepening commitment to socialist ideas or telling her about my sexual explorations and changing girlfriends (she disapproved of most of them). She reminded me that ambi-tious medical men, in Sir William Osler's words, 'put their affec-tions on ice' until at least their forties, when the career had been established. She deplored the hasty wartime marriages that my friends in the forces were making.

She often reminded me of my duty to serve, and to serve well in the army; she believed it was her duty to send her sons forth to battle and often quoted with approval Kipling's poem 'The Egg Shell' where the witch of the north (England) sends forth her sons (the submariners) in their egg shell boats with the words, 'Go sink, she said, or swim, she said, It's all you will get from me!' She never once begged me to take care of myself or expressed fear that I might die or be wounded in the hazards ahead.

1941, 1942, 1943 were the dreary and desperate years of the war. Although there had been no invasion of Britain in 1940, the Germans were everywhere triumphant. They swept through east-ern Europe and down to the Mediterranean. Rommel swept

14

through north Africa and was at the gates of Alexandria. Hitler attacked Russia in the summer of 1941 and his armies reached the outskirts of Moscow and Leningrad. In December 1941 the Japanese entered the war and easily took all East Asia, Hong Kong, Indochina, Malaysia, the Dutch East Indies. In one day two of the navy's greatest warships, the *Prince of Wales* and the *Repulse*, were sunk by Japanese aeroplanes and soon after the 'impregnable fortress' of Singapore fell. In the winter of 1941 there seemed no prospect that we could ever win; but we had to go on fighting because conquest by the Nazis was unthinkable.

I became increasingly guilty about my protected 'reserved' status as a medical student, living at home in safety, getting on with my career when most of my contemporaries were suffering in the forces. Many of us felt this, but I felt it particularly keenly.

I had had two dear friends at school, Denys Barnes and Peter Cheyne, with whom I had wandered the Lothian countryside, camping, bird nesting, fishing and planning our conquests of the world. Both left school when I did, in 1937, and went to University, but chose arts subjects. When the war came they were called up. Denys volunteered for the Fleet Air Arm and became a navy pilot. He was lost in the Mediterranean in 1941, flying an antiquated seaplane against powerful Italian warships. Peter was called up into the Royal Scots and was shipped out to Hong Kong in 1940. When the Japanese overran the colony in 1941 he was wounded and later died in a prisoner of war camp.

By 1942 both of them were dead, and I was comfortably on my way to qualification as a doctor. One way of assuaging the guilt was military work. A Home Guard unit of medical students was formed and I, with my previous OTC training, was made a sergeant. I drilled and practised my fellow students and instructed them in unarmed combat.

Our discomfort about our privileged position was so great that in 1942 a group of us approached the professors with a request that we be allowed to qualify early to get into the army. The dean said it was not possible but Gus, Dan and I spent a weekend redrafting the final year syllabus and finally won permission for a group of 30 (out of the class of 120) to go forward to the finals six months early. In January 1943 I qualified as a doctor.

Young doctors were being called rapidly into the forces, so that the civilian hospitals were very short of staff. In the summer of 1942 James Learmonth, the formidable professor of surgery, had asked me to do a month for him as a 'student resident' in the professorial surgery ward. When I qualified in January 1943 he took me in as his house surgeon – a great honour, but desperately hard work. The medical staff was very short, and the demands for civilian surgery as great as ever. For six months I worked harder than I had ever done in my life (or would ever do again). Days of 14 to 16 hours of toil and operating, and once a week, Thursday to Friday, an 'on take' period of 24 hours when I had no sleep at all. My work deteriorated and I know that patients suffered. But I certainly learned simple surgery and was doing my own operations by the end of that time.

Then in July 1943 it came to an end. After a brief rest, I received my call-up papers telling me to report to the Royal Army Medical Corps college at Crookham in Surrey.

The home situation had settled somewhat. My mother had achieved a standstill in her pulmonary tuberculosis to the astonishment of her doctors. She simply announced 'It is my duty to live until all my children are into university,' and she achieved that aim. By 1943 my sister Gwen had started in medicine at Edinburgh University and the two younger ones, Ralph and June, were nearing the end of their schooling. I felt I could go off to the army in good conscience; anyway my mother would have countenanced no other course.

The war was going rather better. Midwinter 1942–3 had been the turning point, with the Battles of El Alamein when the Afrika Korps were routed and driven back from Egypt, and Stalingrad when a quarter of a million Germans and a field marshal were surrounded, destroyed or taken into captivity. We believed now that we would win the war – some day – but it seemed it would be a very long time, many years at least. We heard, too, that Hitler had 'secret weapons' that would change everything and ensure Germany's victory.

However, the invasion of Europe, for which many of us had clamoured in 1942 with cries of 'Open the second front now', seemed further off than ever. British armies were still being

16

defeated; in Burma by the Japanese, at Dieppe by the Germans. There was need for me in the army and plenty to do!

BECOMING A SOLDIER

So, at last, in July 1943 the moment came for which I had been preparing, one way and another, since 1936; I was a doctor, and an army officer. I was ready to play my part in the Crusade against Fascism. I was a lieutenant RAMC – as father had been in 1915 – and I was even wearing part of his uniform; his ancient much polished Sam Browne belt. My mother was very pleased and had a photo taken of me in my new uniform.

I had no idea what sort of medical work I would be given to do in the army, nor had I any clear aim except that of doing my best. I knew – or thought I knew – quite a lot about the army. I had trained in the Cambridge Officer Training Corps during 1938 and '39 as an artillery officer; I had been a Home Guard sergeant for several years. All the years of my adult life I had been seeing films, reading articles and hearing lectures about war – the Spanish war, the Dunkirk debacle, the campaigns in north Africa, Italy and Russia. I believed that our armies were, as in 1914–18, 'Lions led by donkeys' – brave citizen soldiers mishandled by antiquated warriors and defenders of a vanishing order like Low's Colonel Blimp. I believed that we, the new, the young, the citizen soldiers could do much better and I was one of those who would prove it.

The Royal Army Medical College at Crookham was a pleasant surprise. Our intake were all young doctors, fresh from house jobs, only recently qualified and the college took the task of making us into effective medical officers seriously. Amongst my intake were several class mates from Edinburgh; Dan Cunningham, Graham Falconer, John Tulloch. The instructors were doctors, not much older than ourselves, who had distinguished themselves in the early campaigns of the war. The course commandant was a colonel of 35 who had just returned having escaped from a prisoner of war camp in Italy. We were taught about the army and its organisation and all the tasks we might have – in army hospitals, at battalions or in field ambulances. We had simple field training, being taught the use of maps and compass, which I already knew. There was lots of physical training (PT) morning and evening; I even took extra PT to get myself fitter!

We speculated continuously on where we might be sent and how to get what we wanted. The critical episode, for me, however, was a visit by Colonel McEwen to recruit doctors as parachutists. He made a great impression on us – a glittering military figure – glistening riding boots, red beret, the red collar tabs of a staff officer, a chestful of medals, RAF wings on his chest and parachute wings on his shoulder. Yet, he told us, he was a doctor, and was looking for young men like us to work with him. I described him in a letter to my mother on 28 August 1943:

Probably the major event of the week was the visit of Col. McEwen ADMS of the Airborne Division to see volunteers. He is an amazing man. He is a qualified doctor and also has been a practising lawyer. In the last war he rose to be a squadron leader in the R.F.C. and won the D.F.C. In this war, after various jobs he is now the senior parachutist doctor. He is short, squarely built and looks very fit.He is clean shaven with a long formidable face and truly piercing eyes and curious slight lisp. He was dressed in a very well cut uniform with glistening riding boots, and smoked steadily.

He saw a group of about 25 volunteers, and told us what he wanted. He told us of the work we should do and it sounded both useful and interesting. He has just been in battle in Tunisia where they did 162 surgical operations in one day. There have apparently been plenty other such shows (it is said there is a D.S.O. and bar coming through for him for what he did there). He saw us all individually and then called in a group of 10, of whom I had the good fortune to be one, and told us that he had accepted us. He then stood there and scrutinized us. It was amazing. Ten of us, large useful lads, all qualified doctors and men with minds of their own and he held us petrified as a cobra holds a rabbit. He told us to relax and no one moved a muscle. He first scrutinized us one after the other, and then stood and talked to us about our work and the sort of people he wanted and pointed out three who he thought were the most likely of us, just by things that he saw in our faces – a trouble here, and a dreamy look there. He will be letting us know within the next few days whether he wants us immediately or whether we go on the waiting list. But even if it is the waiting list it is expected that we will be in by Xmas. So I am now fairly definitely fixed up.

After four weeks at Crookham, we had a week at the Army School of Hygiene at Mytchett – a much duller place – where we were taught about the many ways to rid men of lice and how to build, operate and inspect latrines and cook-houses. At the end of the course I received my posting notice to 225 Parachute Field Ambulance in the 6th Airborne Division. I had been accepted to be a parachutist!

I spent two weeks at 225 before going off on the parachute training course. They were only notable for two events – a training march of 60 miles in 30 hours, when one third of the unit became casualties (mostly with blisters) but which I (to my surprise and delight) completed without difficulty, and a mess party when Colonel McEwen visited our unit, drank an immense amount of our whisky and told those of us who were just off to the parachute training course terrifying stories of casualties and 'roman candles' (when the parachute failed to open).

Then I departed for Hardwick Hall, near Chesterfield with a group of RAMC orderlies and conscientious objectors who had recently arrived at 225. The four weeks at Hardwick were a 'toughening' course, designed to make volunteers from all over the army fit enough for parachuting. On 30 September 1943 I wrote:

I have just finished one week here and am starting the second now. I am stronger and tougher than I have ever been before and also rather tired! We do P.T. and long distance marches, cliff climbing, gym, boxing and such like all day. It is all most excellently planned so as to leave us at the end of the day very tired, but not aching anywhere. There are a number of tests which one has to pass: when I came here I thought I should never be able to pass them at all, but after this last week I realise that I may get through them after all.

During this time we were coming to take pride in ourselves as an elite. We had lectures on the achievements and traditions of the parachutists – 'Red Devils' – as we were taught to call ourselves. We heard of their deeds in battle, particularly in north Africa and Sicily. We learned special songs which we sang with drunken gusto. In the evenings our instructors told us tales of great figures of the past, and the heroes of the First Parachute Battalion and 1st Brigade who fought so well in North Africa.

Then, from Hardwick, we went to Ringway, an aerodrome outside Manchester for our parachute training. For a week, RAF instructors made us jump through a variety of holes and doors on the command 'action stations – go!' until we responded quite automatically. They taught us to roll on landing, which came easy to me because of my judo training but which many found difficult.

Then we went to Tatton Park for our first parachute drop, from a captive balloon. The first parachute jump is a great moment for most people, and for many a great thrill and an enduring memory. Even now, many years later, it is vivid in my mind, especially the clear delight of that sunlit autumn day, the singing of a distant lark, the moment of blissful peace, as well as the high elation after completion. I wrote an account of it in a letter to my mother – (22 October 1943).

Well, the worst is over. I have jumped, and there is (comparatively speaking) nothing to it. We arrived here last Saturday and for 5 days did 'synthetic' training – i.e. jumping through mock apertures onto mats, swinging on swings, practising falls etc. Most of this was rather dull, but quite essential, as one may land at speeds up to 25 m.p.h. or even more on special occasions, and one has to jump, with a large parachute on through a hole about 4 ft diameter and not touch any of the sides. The only fearsome thing in the ground training was the 'fan' – where you jump off a platform 35 feet up suspended by nothing but a wire as thin as a pencil. This is wound on a fan and your weight makes the fan revolve and the air resistance breaks your fall. 35 feet is a long way to jump in cold blood, and on this my fear of heights gave me some worry. In the balloon this fear disappeared entirely. At 600 feet the effect of height was quite lost. The ground looks like an aerial photo, or a scale model: I had no fear of it at all.

On Saturday morning we did our first balloon jump. In a way I was quite disappointed, for I had prepared myself to overcome a considerable dose of that fear of heights that kept me from mountain climbing, and that has frequently unmanned me badly. There was no need: there was no vertigo at all! As far as I can see, the fear that has to be overcome is imaginative fear – fear of the 'chute not opening etc, and such fears I have always been well able to overcome. I can remember when Denys and Peter and I used to play 'dares' if it was a question of physical performance I was poor, and if it was a matter of height climbing I was bad, where it was a fear of human possibilities – such as pilfering a garden – I was as good as the rest.

To return to the balloon: I looked out as we went up and saw the cows shrink down to little blobs, and the people to dots, and then we came to a pause. The cage rocked gently and a slight breeze blew around us. The sun, which was hidden below now shone on us, and everything was quiet, and separate from the complicated earth. Then I got my order. 'Action Stations No. 1' – I put my legs in the hole 'Go!' – and as I had done some two or three hundred times to the same command during the last week, I went. There followed one moment that was really and truly quite lovely. I felt cool sweet morning air rushing up past me, and felt quite detached from everything; just there, alone and unattached in middle air, with my heels firmly together and my fists clutching my trousers. Then there was a rustling crackle overhead, and I looked up and saw the canopy, mottled brown and green open out, close partly, and finally assume its taut position above me. As it did so I took hold of my lift webs, gently but firmly, and I began to swing, no longer blissfully unattached. Then I began the series of manoeuvres in which I had been trained. I grasped the forward lift web and pulled down: I regarded the ground: it was far away: I paid heed to the megaphone's instructions and bent my knees a little more, relaxed, looked at my canopy. I then glanced at the ground again. It was near, far too near, and was rushing past at great speed. I was going to land backwards – no sideways – no forwards – heavens, I had not pulled on my lift webs – quick – and then it hit me. Not forwards as I expected but sideways and backwards. I did not take enough shock on my feet and came down on my hip with a bang; rolled over, saw the 'chute collapse, and I was there. It was all over. A moment of flatness was followed by a happy elation, the natural aftermath of the recent tension, and the doubts and questioning of the last 2 months. This elation sustained me through the coming days as we did further balloon jumps, one night balloon jump and several aircraft jumps, a total of eight training jumps.

In the mess in the evening, and as we hung about the hangars waiting to go, we began to hear about the frightening side of parachuting such as the 'roman candle' when the parachute fails to open and the luckless soldier plunges to his death. Our instructors assured us that if we followed their instructions we could not possibly come to harm, but we had our doubts. We heard of high winds that broke bones, of broken ankles, wrists, collar bones, concussion. We sang the macabre songs of parachuting disasters. Several people decided it was too much for them and left the course to 'return to their units'. We heard that we could withdraw up till the last jump, but that if we 'jibbed' after getting our 'wings' we would be court martialled and sent to prison.

Then, we had completed our eight jumps! We were presented with our wings and rushed to sew them onto the shoulders of our tunics before we went home, on 'jump leave' wearing our brand new red berets for our admiring mothers and girlfriends. My mother had another photo taken of me! At that time parachute wings and red berets were comparatively rare, and old friends and fellow doctors still doing their house jobs were frankly envious.

23

Physically more fit than I had ever been in my life, erect and proud, I strode round in my khaki uniform and my bright red beret. At this stage I felt very pleased with myself. In three months I had not only become a medical officer and a soldier, but a member of a *corps d'elite.*

225 PARACHUTE FIELD AMBULANCE

After my leave I went back to 225, where I found that I was to be the 'supernumerary officer' – ready to take the place of any doctor who became a casualty during the unit's training. I remained with them until they took off for D-Day on 6 June 1944 some eight months later.

This was for me a long and painful period in which I was made fully aware of my insignificance and general unworthiness, a verdict on my uselessness to the army with which, in retrospect, I have to agree.

225 (Parachute) Field Ambulance was an experimental unit, unusual in many ways. The first British parachute operations in 1940 and 1941 had been very small, a few score soldiers, and the battalion medical officers had provided necessary medical treatment. When the numbers involved in parachute operations increased, the proper care of the wounded became a challenge, so the parachute field ambulances were developed. In the North African campaign of 1942 there was first one parachute field ambulance (led by Colonel MacEwen) with the first parachute brigade and later three field ambulances, each attached to one of the three brigades of the first Airborne Division. They fought in Tunisia, in Sicily and in Italy. Parachute field ambulances consisted of doctors (medical officers) and nursing orderlies, all trained RAMC; they also had a surgical team of two surgeons and operating room staff capable of doing major operations. The unit went in with the fighting troops, set up field dressing stations and were expected to treat all casualties until relieved by the advancing ground troops.

This was the task – but it was all new in 1943. There had only been one British campaign using more than one battalion of parachutists (in Sicily) and many things had gone wrong there. So 225 was full of planning and argument. There were long discussions of what each of us should carry, what should be in the containers and which medical equipment could stand being dropped from an aeroplane. Doctors from the First Airborne Division came to talk to us about what they had learned.

225 Parachute Field Ambulance had other unusual characteristics because of the way it was raised. The core was a territorial army field ambulance from Sheffield, prewar volunteers who had been turned into an airborne unit and invited to volunteer for parachuting. Only a few had accepted the opportunity! Then there were parachute volunteers from RAMC units from all of the British army. In 1943 the only way to get away from many units of the army was to volunteer for parachuting. As a result 225 (and the whole division) had a fine collection of malcontents from all over the army – all brave, some excellent soldiers, but many chronic misfits. To them were added medical officers like myself, newly qualified doctors who knew nothing of the army but whose keenness and enthusiasm led them to volunteer for parachuting.

However, the army had not been able to persuade enough RAMC medical orderlies to volunteer for parachuting and had turned to another special group of men – the conscientious objectors of the Non Combatant Corps (NCC). When conscription had started at the beginning of the war, some young men objected on conscientious grounds to killing other people. Most were Christians who believed that Christ meant what he said about not killing; some came from sects, such as the Quakers, who had a long stated policy of non violence. In World War I conscientious objectors had been reviled as 'conchies', stigmatized and sent to prison but in our war the army authorities were rather more imaginative. They created the Non Combatant Corps and allowed conscientious objectors to enrol in it.

At first in 1939 the NCC had been employed on dull and menial tasks, but they pressed for more useful things to do. They asked to be medical orderlies but the army refused, saying that RAMC men had to be prepared to carry arms. Then, in the summer of 1940, the problem of dealing with unexploded German bombs became acute. Men were needed to dig out these bombs which might at any moment explode: a job for volunteers. The army found it difficult to get enough of these, so they offered the job to the Non Combatant Corps; many of the conscientious objectors welcomed the opportunity and served with great bravery and many casualties. By 1943, however, not so many bombs were being dropped on Britain and the bomb disposal units were idle.

To get more parachute medical orderlies the army offered men of the NCC the opportunity to volunteer for parachuting and be medical orderlies, and many of them accepted. They were delighted because at last they were being trained to do the medical work they had always wanted. They volunteered, trained as parachutists, and came to 225 to learn to be parachute medical orderlies. They were fascinating characters, all brave, many highly educated, some eccentric and many stubborn. They were willing to be led, but refused to be driven.

So 225 was a unit composed of ex-territorials from Sheffield, restless individuals from all over the army, inexperienced but keen young doctors and a group of seasoned conscientious objectors. To weld this strange collection together into an effective unit, the army chose an interesting character as commanding officer; Colonel E.I. Bruce-Harvey, MB, ChB. Bruce Harvey was a scion of an old landed family who had had an adventurous life. Just too young for service in World War I, he had joined the Royal Navy as a junior officer. Growing bored with that he had resigned and became a junior officer in the Scots Guards. After a scrape he was sent to the West Africa Corps. Then he resigned from the army and became a medical student at Edinburgh, finally qualifying in his forties just before the war broke out. He was thus both a doctor and an experienced soldier. He volunteered for parachuting to get out of a unit he disliked and was picked to weld us together and to take us into battle – a task to which he applied himself with vigour and enthusiasm. Over six feet tall, with a bristling black moustache and beady eyes, he was a figure to strike dread into any laggard, particularly when he let fly one of his notorious tirades. Off duty, however, he was a pleasant companion, a connoisseur of good wines, good food and beautiful women.

The basic unit in a parachute field ambulance was a 'section'

27

consisting of a medical officer, staff sergeant, a corporal and 17 nursing orderlies. They worked together, trained together and would jump into action together. The best job for a junior doctor was to be in charge of a section, but by the time I joined 225 all the section posts were filled. I envied the Section MOs who worked with their men, training them and knitting them into a team.

In October 1943, 225 was stationed on Salisbury Plain in an old army cantonment known as Bulford Lines. The officers lived cramped into houses designed for NCOs families, but in no hardship. Every morning before dawn we ran up Beacon Hill, just above the camp, and our training continued strenuous, though the main thrust was training the teams and preparing the equipment for the big operation expected next year, in 1944.

When I was first with 225 in September before going on my parachute training, Bruce Harvey was quite pleased to have me. I think he was pleased to have the son of one of his teachers under his command; he was also impressed that I was one of the few doctors still on my feet after a thirty mile training route march when a third of the men and half of the officers of his new unit became casualties. When I came back from Ringway, however, things had changed. He had enough medical officers and I was 'supernumerary' – to be available if any of the other medical officers became casualties. Whenever Bruce Harvey was ordered to send an officer on a 'course' he sent me so that the training of the others was not interrupted. I went to Bath on a blood transfusion course, to York on a gas course, to Millbank, London on a hygiene course and to Wales on field firing practice.

I was given the job of being medical officer to the unit. I was responsible for the 'MI room' (Medical Inspection room) and with the assistance of nursing orderly corporal had to hold sick parades every morning. A letter to my mother in December 1943 describes the job and how I felt about it:

I act as the doctor of the unit and take sick parade every morning at 8 a.m. 30–40 men and plenty of hard thinking to do. I look after our men, and a nearby unit of field engineers, and have all the responsibilities and privileges of a Regtl. Medical Officer, while living in a mess of doctors where I can get plenty of help. It is very interesting, and I am learning a good deal of medicine of a particular kind. Anyone who seems to have any disease that I had seen on the wards is at once shot off to a specialist or a hospital, while I concentrate on keeping the others healthy. Blisters, sprains, coughs, 'flus are my stuff, with other odd things thrown. The real delight of it is that unlike civil medicine I have complete control of the patient's environment, and my endeavours are blocked by nothing except my own failings and the patient's personality. I learn a lot this way.

They are an excellent lot of men, and very few scrimshankers. A lot of my business is dealing with the effects of trauma and strain – parachute jumping and 50 mile marches. It is amazing the things that turn up, and the way that any small defect is shown up. My other main job is skin diseases of various kinds. I am getting quite clever at spotting scabies!

While I am doing this I am also doing my full work as an officer in the field ambulance – cross country marching with packs etc. The other day we did a jump from a newer type of aircraft which was much more fun than the old ones we had at Ringway. However the wind was rather high and we hit the ground pretty hard. I got dragged half way across a ploughed field. However no harm resulted.

Over that long first year in the army – from my induction in August 1943 to my first experience of battle in January 1945 – I was being turned, painfully, into a 'medical officer'. Although I wished for the transformation I was also resistant to it, often protesting painfully (and ineffectually). I was reacting to the whole ethos and way of life of this army, so many of whose ideas were alien to me, I was reacting to the emerging culture of the parachutists, and I was reacting to two groups; the officers and the men of 225.

Until we went into action most of my interactions with the men were formalized by the army discipline. They had to salute and call me 'sir'. I talked to them briskly and usually formally. Even in the MI room, where I was treating their illnesses and complaints, the army and its pressures were always there. Almost every diagnosis led to disciplinary consequences. Bad blisters meant being excused boots, route marches, sentry duty. A fever meant admission to the military hospital. Scabies meant disinfestation and stoppage of leave. So medical examination was a wary encounter between a sufferer seeking relief and an officer who might be able to treat suffering but could also remove privileges. I often wondered what the men were making of the army experience, but in those early days no one would have been so foolish as to tell me.

Relations in the officers' mess was different. These were my peers; and amongst them I would find my friends (if any). In a field ambulance mess nearly all the officers were doctors; in a parachute field ambulance they were nearly all young doctors. Most of them had qualified in the last year, as I had, and we had many common experiences. Some like Tommy Wilson and Bobby Marquis had been at Edinburgh with me. Others, like Gordon Kennedy, David Tibbs, John Wagstaffe and Ray Kirkham had been at London hospitals. We had common acquaintances and common experiences. Slightly more senior were the two surgeons, Peter Essex-Lopresti and Henry Daintree-Johnston and the second in command, Dennis Thomson. The only non-medical members of the mess were the Roman Catholic padre for the brigade, Father Bristow, the transport officer, Leslie Hill and the quartermaster. We were all very fit, and many had been sportsmen; we all had in common the experience of parachute training, with its fears and delights. None of us were regulars, except the quartermaster. All the others, even the colonel, were 'hostilities only' officers, doing what had to be done, fitting in with the ways of the army, and trying to work out how to be an effective unit in unknown and unguessable operations.

I fitted poorly into this group – garrulous, naive, argumentative, I talked too much and put people's teeth on edge, but some others were also awkward and we had to put up with one another for we knew we would go into action together and at any moment one's life might depend on a man whose table manners were lamentable, whose religious and political views were intolerable, and who had seemed a fool and a bore!

At 225 I did not have much to do, but plenty of time to talk – which I did to everyone's irritation. The colonel had several occasions to reprimand me, and I still recall one of his 'bollockings' (as his rages were called) which started with a detailed examination of my failing on a task and ended with his bellowing, so that all in the office could hear, 'You're a very junior officer, Mr Clark, with an unwarrantably high opinion of yourself!' To which I could only assent, 'Yes, sir', before he bellowed, 'Get out!'

I gradually learned to get on superficially with most people and to chat in the superficial way that was appropriate – avoiding literature or politics or religion or deep feelings – anything that might open any deep rift. We got drunk and grumbled about the army, about our pay, about delays in getting leave, about the colonel and his unfairness. I tried to find kindred spirits, but seldom succeeded. Gordon Kennedy, a research physiologist from London, shared my political leanings and I had some good talks with him before he was posted out to a battalion. I often felt very lonely.

At one period the medical officer of the 7th Battalion fell sick and I was sent out to act as battalion medical officer for two weeks. This was a new world for me and I described it in a letter to my mother dated 30 April 1944:

I am living in an entirely different atmosphere just now. I have left the Field Ambulance and am living with one of the parachute battalions as Regimental Medical Officer. The living is rather more comfortable, but the atmosphere is entirely different and Philistine. I have yet to see anyone reading a book! They all live a hard active life by day, and either sleep, chat or go out in the evening. It is so different from our mess where nearly everyone reads a good deal, and there are interesting conversations every now and then. I am not too oppressed by the Philistines, for the mess is large enough for me to keep on my own, and they are not intolerant. They are all, of course, very young. The Colonel is, I should think, about 35, the Majors are about 25–30, and the Captains and subalterns mostly younger than me! I feel quite an aged and responsible man.

My own position, again, is entirely different. In the field ambulance I am just the most junior member of the mess, possessing a stock of knowledge and training common to the oth-

31

ers, and judged by my military competence and my personality. Here I am 'the doc'. I may or may not have a pleasant type of personality and be able to fit in with the others. That matters a little socially. But the important thing is that I am a separate being. I have special knowledge, special functions, black arts. I can mark people off or on duty and none can criticise. I am the only doctor and my position is fixed. I do not fail, or get put on the carpet – as the other officers do – nor do I rise. I am never anything more than the doctor. I would never take command or give another officer an order.

It is an interesting position, and is of course, one that is new to me, since I have passed the last six years of my life entirely in the company of medics. It is in a way an intoxicating position. I have great power; no one can criticise my methods unless disaster occurs. I can experiment with ideas, and carry out any queer ideas I may have. I can rearrange things as I will. But on the other hand, it has great limitations. I can do so much, but can go no further. Worst of all is the isolation.

I was unhappy, lonely and uncertain. There were some old friends in the division, such as Dan Cunningham and Bobby Marquis, but they were in other units and I seldom saw them. On every possible weekend I slipped away to London where old friends at University College Hospital arranged parties for me. There I met a delightful girl, Mary Rose Harris, and we soon became lovers. A passionate Cornish rebel, she had run away from home to become a nurse in wartime London. She had endured the ferocious training of University College Hospital and had taken up radical politics. Known amongst the medical students as 'Red Harris' she was beautiful, queenly and passionately involved in the politics of left wing London. I found her delightful and she and her friends were an exhilarating contrast to the officers mess with its endless talk of motors cars, golf and 'bints' at 'smashing parties'.

Apart from Mary Rose, however, there was little good for me about the winter of 1943–44 during which all southern England was preparing for the long awaited invasion of Europe. More and more American troops arrived; the little Hampshire lanes were pounded by vast trucks carrying enormous tanks, which casually smashed the corners off the ancient houses. Every week there were new arrivals, about whom we did not gossip as security became increasingly important.

It was clear that parachutists would lead the invasion; everyone in 225 was actively preparing for their part in it. I had no part, so I was sent off on all the odd jobs. Whenever troops were doing something dangerous, a doctor and an ambulance had to be standing by. I spent many hours sitting on dropping zones when practice jumps were going on or attending firing ranges when live ammunition was being used. I was not always idle; I did quite a lot of emergency first aid when careless people fired off guns or dropped hand grenades.

One episode effectively destroyed the remnants of my belief in the safety of parachuting – a night drop when a following aircraft ploughed among the tops of a line of parachutes chopping them open so that the unfortunate soldiers plunged fatally to earth. It fell to me to collect the warm shattered corpses, every bone broken, and take them to the local mortuary.

I took part in several large drops, including one where 225 was put on a demonstration for some generals. The wind was too high, but they would not cancel. I was concussed, the colonel was knocked out, the regimental sergeant major had his legs broken and one of the men from my Ringway section had his back broken. I was beginning to realise that soldiering was dangerous!

In the spring one of our medical officers moved to a battalion and I was told to take over his section. I was delighted and plunged into a training programme. Some weeks later, however, a tall captain joined us from corps headquarters and I was told to hand my section over to him. It was said that he was a high flyer, a regular, an outstanding doctor who had a key post at headquarters, but that he had been told that he had no chance of promotion until he had seen action, so he had come to 225 as a section officer. To me he was most courteous, but I felt very bitter. It was back to duty on dropping zones and field firing ranges again and postings to any irrelevant course that came along.

The invasion drew nearer and we knew that the airborne division had a major part to play. Everyone seemed to have a task but me. I pleaded with the colonel and with Colonel McEwen to be allowed to go with the others. For a few days I was attached to the group of engineers who were to make the *coup-de-main* attack on the Arne bridge but then I was replaced by a more senior doctor. The division went into sealed transit camps near the airfields for the last ten days briefing, and my job was to man the first aid tent and deal with minor injuries!

In the early days of June the weather changed and the wind rose. They were originally to take off in the evening of 4 June but there was a gale blowing and the invasion was postponed. The next night was little better, but they had to go. My task was to be at the airfield and attend the casualties as the battered aircraft came back from France. Afterwards a small group of us 'rear party' trailed forlornly back to Bulford. I felt very low as the following extracts from letters to mother show:

8 June 1944
This note begins with an apology. I am not in France. I am still in Britain – please do not disinherit me on the spot! I did not jib on the day!

You remember I mentioned I was landing all the odd jobs: well I also landed the job of staying behind and looking after things, damn it! I went to the camp with the lads, saw them through all their final training, and said goodbye to them on the airfield; and then came back here, to deserted billets. It is a very long time since I felt so sick at heart – probably the last time was when I missed the Rockefeller.

There they were – the lads I had lived with and trained with for six months: whom I had seen grow from a muddle of individuals to a first class unit – going off in magnificent spirit – singing and joking, with red roses and flowers on their helmets – and I was left behind.

And now I sit here and listen to the reports come in. As you saw in the papers 6th Airborne Division are in the Caen district and forging ahead. And I am not with them. It girns me continually, and yet I have to be philosophic and not get silly about it. I am feeling better than I did a day or so ago. When or if I shall join them I do not know. I can only wait and see.

I still sit here cleaning up odd bits and pieces, a melancholy life. What the outlook is I do not know. We merely know, as you do, that the lads are having a lot of heavy fighting, and presume that casualties must be high.

Life here is peculiar and unsatisfactory. Everything is haunted by the memory of the people away, and it lies at the back of all conversation. The men left behind are mostly duds, scrimshankers and unfit. Some of the officers are that sort, too, though most of them are like myself, fit men held back, and furious at their ill fortune. The combatants find it very difficult to bear this with any degree of philosophy (they have probably never heard of philosophy) and are consequently having a series of rather dull drinking parties. The parties are dull again because of the shadow in the background. Nearly all the women that come to them – V.A.D.s and the like – are awaiting word from someone over there. Thus the whole thing is most melancholy . . .

As it happened, it was a good thing I did not go to France. My gloom did not lift and I began to feel ill and nauseated. Then one morning in the shaving mirror I saw that my eyes were bright yellow; I was suffering from jaundice. I was moved to an army hospital, where I spent the whole of July 1944, quite seriously ill with hepatitis. The whole ward was ringing with the tales of the great invasion. The ward radio was going constantly and there was much about the dash and bravery of the Red Devils who had led the attack. My jaundiced gloom deepened steadily; I felt useless, hopeless, a failure. One of the few consolations were Mary Rose's visits. She came down to see me from London, emptied by flying bombs.

This was the time of Hitler's 'secret weapons'. The first VIs, the pilotless planes which we called 'buzz bombs', were on 16 May. London was once again evacuated and only the brave and the busy remained. Mary Rose, as a nurse, was in the midst of it and my visits to her became perilous. I several times later heard a VI, put-putting across the sky like a motor bike – then waited in anxiety when the engine stopped and I knew the flying bomb was going down on someone else.

In due course my liver recovered and my jaundice lifted. I had a brief period of sick leave at home in Edinburgh and then went back to Bulford in early August where I found a small group of men looking after the unit's huts and stores, idle and demoralized. None of us had much to do and we were all dispirited. My sick bay corporal decided he had had enough of parachuting and 'jibbed' at a practice jump. It was not a surprise to me; he had informed me of his intention, and the refusal was ritualised. However, he had to be court martialled and sent off to army prison, the 'glass house'.

Again my main consolation was Mary Rose who would come down for periods of leave to Marlborough; I would slip away there in a jeep provided by our accommodating transport sergeant, a professional criminal in civilian life. The battles in Normandy ground on for several months but then the great breakthrough came and the allied tanks rushed across France.

In September 6th Airborne Division returned triumphant from Normandy and 225 came with them. They had distinguished themselves in bitter fighting. There had been many medical casualties in Normandy. The regular from headquarters, who had taken my section, had been killed, which put an end to his ambitions. Several other doctors had been killed or wounded and David Tibbs and Tommy Wilson had been moved to battalions. The unit was filled up with a new intake, including green young medical officers. I was now a captain (an automatic promotion after 12 months) and apparently rather more useful. Colonel Bruce Harvey had been decorated with a DSO and promoted, and the second in command, Major Hewlings, took over as colonel. He was a friendly man whom I did not fear so much.

At last I was given a section and started a training programme. I had Staff Sergeant Smart to guide me, a massive taciturn Welshman and former boxing champion, a regular RAMC nursing orderly with lots of experience of the army and its ways, Corporal Shobbrook, a steady Englishman, and 17 others, some experienced men from Normandy, a number of conscientious objectors and some new recruits to parachuting. A particular friend was Harry Abbot, a delightful gentle architect and singer. I felt much more at ease in 225. I had a job to do and an assured place; I was an accepted member of the unit, though of course not a veteran of battle as most of them were.

The summer of 1944 had been a glorious one for the British and Americans. After so many delays, the armies had landed in Europe. The tricky D-Day landing in June had been a success. After desperate fighting in Normandy the German resistance had been broken and their tanks and armies had fled. Paris fell and then Brussels. It seemed that the war would be 'over by Christmas'. Then in September came a check that was a major shock for us in the airborne forces.

All summer we had known that our senior colleagues, the 1st Airborne Division, the veterans of north Africa, were sitting in East Anglia, impatient to join the victorious advance. Suddenly they were thrown into an ambitious operation to capture all the bridges over the lower Rhine – the biggest airborne operation there had ever been.

For a week we listened to the news, at first with excitement and then with dismay as it became clear that our comrades were being defeated. The escape of the remnants of the battered division who had dropped to capture the furthest bridge at Arnhem was hailed in the newspapers as a triumph, but we soon learned what an appalling disaster it had been – three quarters of the division killed, wounded and captured. More frightening, we heard that all the doctors had had to go into captivity with the wounded they were treating. We had always accepted that we doctors might have to go into captivity with our wounded patients, but for all the doctors of an entire division, nine parachute field ambulances, all the RAMC men, even the divisional medical chief, to become prisoners in the battle, that was something we had never considered.

As time went on we learned how many of our friends and colleagues had been killed or severely wounded. Later further details began to come through, of reckless bravery, but also gross inefficiency. Not a single wireless set in the division had worked! No one in England knew what they were doing or could help them. Medical supplies ran out; errors were made in surgical priorities. We went through a sad and sober period and re-examined our

37

methods of organising our work and packing our equipment. By now we knew that parachuting into action was a dangerous and nasty business.

In November I took Mary Rose up to Edinburgh to meet my mother, who, to my relief, approved of her – recognising another outspoken rebel – and we became officially engaged.

As the winter settled, so did the war. Bitter fighting went on in the estuaries of the Scheldt and the forests up to the Rhine, but there were no major operations on the western front. Liberated France was settling down with stories of bitter revenge and savage justice. The allied armies were consolidating and preparing for the spring offensive. In the east the Russians were mounting winter offensives and pushing into Poland. Everyone felt sure that the Germans were beaten and that all that would be needed would be a good push in the spring.

At 225 we were getting on with our training, route marching and parachute drops and replanning our kit and packing in the light of Normandy experiences and what we were beginning to learn about the Arnhem disaster. It was clear that major airborne operations needed fairly good weather, so that we knew we would not be needed before spring. We prepared for a massive Christmas celebration, buying in turkeys, barrels of beer and many other goodies.

A TRAINED SOLDIER

By the end of 1944, therefore, I appeared to be a 'trained soldier' – a doctor who had been turned into a competent medical officer. I was a member of an experienced battle proven unit, equipped and ready for a great airborne operation. But how did I feel, inside myself?

Although I was 24 and had been a qualified doctor for two years, and an army officer for a year and half, I was still essentially romantic and naive. It was not that my life had been unduly sheltered. As a medical student, doctor and accident officer, I had seen wounding and pain and death. Nor had I been shielded from personal blows; I had lost my father at 21, I had seen my mother through mortal illness, I had suffered major personal disappointments. I was no longer as sexually immature as I had been on graduation; I had a lover and was now engaged to marry.

But somehow none of these had touched the essential romantic core. I saw the world in simple colours. We were engaged in a crusade against evil; Nazism, with its race theories, its reactionary political creed, its bigotry and its drive to dominate the world was something to be fought and destroyed, a dragon for our times. I was one of those privileged to be active in slaying the dragon. I saw myself, too, in a doomed romantic light; I knew that I was going to die in battle. I knew that we were fighting for a finer, better, more equal, more kindly England, the socialist England that would be built after the war was over, but I knew that I would not be part of it. Although I had vaguely considered a possible later medical career, I never thought much about what I would do after the war or how I would fit in to the post-war world. If I had been told that I would have a full professional career, beget children

39

and grandchildren and live past the age of 70, I would have laughed in amazement.

The year 1945 was to shake and challenge my beliefs. It was going to bring me in touch with great and awful doings – victory and conquest, defeat and degradation, refugees, concentration camps, revolution and civil war. It was going to show me how complex and unpredictable human affairs were, and that nothing was easy or straightforward. It was to show me vividly many of my own weaknesses, limitations and failings and finally perhaps leave me sufficiently chastened to become a doctor.

My main preoccupations in 1944 were to try to do a good job, to meet the expectation of the army, the unit and the men of my section whom I had to lead into battle, to be an effective officer and leader, and to be a competent doctor. My fear was of failing in that task; of letting my men down, of letting the unit down, of showing incompetence, fear, or cowardice. I wondered how I should manage in battle; would I become useless, frightened, anxious, jittery, or worse, a 'battle exhaustion case'? I feared I would let down my mother, my family, myself.

I was, of course, also afraid of being injured or killed. I knew now that parachuting was dangerous and chancy and I realised that battle was worse. Death did not seem so frightening, for that was the end, but painful wounding, mutilation, crippling seemed terrible – and quite likely.

By now I felt I knew the army fairly well, and I had seen something of our American allies; extravagant, exotic young men. But I knew little of the people we were fighting – our enemies, the Germans, and even less of the Japanese.

In Germany in 1935 and 1936, I had met many Germans who had been kind and friendly to me; I had also met Germans who had been nasty to me. I knew well enough that Germans, like the Scots and the English, were a mixed bunch, some friendly, some nasty. I never met a wicked German – but then I had never at that time met real wickedness in the Scots or the English. Spite, envy, malice perhaps, but never wholehearted wickedness or cruelty, or enduring, consuming hatred.

I had studied German at school for five years and spoke it fluently, if clumsily. I had, however, hated Nazism when I had first

40

encountered it in 1936. There had followed several years of left wing propaganda telling of fascist atrocities, followed by five years of official British government propaganda, articles, news-reels and films all telling how evil our enemies were and how good, brave, courteous, chivalrous and gentle our own soldiers were.

I had of course only half believed the propaganda, for there was the healthy corrective of the scepticism of my father and my uncle Robert Mennell, the pacifist orator, who had spent three years in British gaols between 1915 and 1918 for his pacifist principles. Both warned me to doubt atrocity stories particularly those put out by the government.

The Nazis had put their political opponents in concentration camps when they came to power in 1933, and we had been told many tales of their brutality. There had been rumours in 1943 and 1944 of mass killings by the Nazis but these came mostly from Russian sources and were suspect. I had not seen or talked to a German (other than anti-Nazi refugees) for five years. I did not know what I would find, nor what I should think. So my ideas in 1944 about the Germans were a curious mixture of half believed propaganda, checked by scepticism, memories of my own experiences of German people and a lively curiosity.

Of our other enemies, the Japanese, I knew much less. I had read reports and books and seen films about these terrifying yellow warriors, who had conquered all the East, had sunk the British navy and the American navy, reduced the fortress of Singapore with ease, captured Burma and swept to the edges of Australia and India. There had been several years of fighting reported from strangely named Pacific islands; Guadalcanal, Truk, Kwajalein, and it seemed that the Americans, at least, could fight the Japanese on equal terms. But what the Japanese were actually like, I did not know. I knew of *Madam Butterfly* and *The Mikado* and I knew that Baden Powell in 1910 had praised the 'plucky little Japs'. But it was all a muddle of tales and fables. I knew nothing directly of them, and in 1944 I had no expectation of meeting them.

41

INTO BATTLE AT LAST

December 1944 was cold and wet but most of us in Britain were feeling fairly relaxed. The great invasion had been accomplished; France and Belgium were free. The VIs and V2s had stopped falling on London. Clearly the Germans were beaten; it was only a matter of mopping up in the spring. The Sixth Airborne was training for its spring operation but most of us were more interested in preparing for our Christmas celebrations and the possibility of leave in the New Year. The quartermaster had bought turkeys and plum puddings and beer; the officers' and sergeants' messes had laid in large stocks of liquor.

Suddenly, Hitler surprised us all with his astonishing winter offensive in the Ardennes, later known as the 'Battle of the Bulge'. This opened in secret and the news of it was at first suppressed, so it took us in 225 entirely by surprise.

Our first inkling was at a mess party on 20 December when, unusually, the colonel and the adjutant were called out from the drinking by a messenger from division. When we got back to the unit, rather drunk, all officers were called in to the colonel's office – something was going on in Europe and we were wanted! We had 48 hours to prepare to go into action by land. For two hectic days we packed and repacked all our kit: our personal kit, the section's medical kit and all the goods of the unit. We packed kitbags 'to follow on with the baggage party' but knew we might have to manage with only what we carried.

On 23 December we were put into lorries and driven all through the night, then embarked at Folkestone on a ferry to cross the Channel. We set off – and then stopped. The ship put down its anchors and there we remained for 24 hours. There was little food except biscuits and tea. It was Christmas Day, and we thought bitterly of all the turkeys and beer we had left behind. It was a brilliant winter's day and we were in 'The Downs' – the traditional anchorage – from which we could easily see the sunlit English coast. The boat, of course, was full of rumours. It was known that the Germans had mounted some sort of surprise attack, and that the parachutists were to stop them. We were told that they had also mined the Channel and that was why we could not cross. Certainly there were many small navy boats scurrying about on the sea, and many planes overhead. Finally the anchor was raised and we zig-zagged across the Channel. We disembarked in the dark in a shattered port and climbed into lorries which drove all through the night. As morning broke we crossed the Meuse – a wide dull grey river running between snow-covered banks – and were then sent off in different directions. My section and I found ourselves in a small Ardennes village in a requisitioned cafe. It was bitterly cold, snow and ice everywhere, twenty degrees of frost, and all the windows in the village had been shattered when the bridge had been blown up three days earlier. The villagers were sour, dour and frightened. They had heard that the Germans might be on them again soon. There were a few British troops, mostly line of communications men, who knew little about what was happening – except that everything was a 'SNAFU' (situation normal, all fouled up). We wondered and waited.

Not for long; we were ordered forward, and I was told to set up a dressing station in the village of Resteigne. The Germans were in the next village, Bure, and were to be attacked the next day. Companies and platoons of the 13th Parachute Battalion, many of whom I knew personally, came marching though the village for the assault, full of cheerful confidence. Sherman tanks rumbled through, massive and effective looking; the drivers were Hussars who had fought them all the way up from Normandy. The tanks looked like tinkers' caravans, with cooking pots, wine flagons, bed rolls and miscellaneous loot dangling from the camouflage netting.

We took over a cafe as our dressing station. This was the first time I had set up an aid post in action, so I left it to the veterans in my section. They rapidly smashed the plate glass windows, then cleared the furniture from the rooms, either by piling it up against the windows or throwing it into the street. Shells were beginning to fall on the village and a building opposite was hit and collapsed. Our first casualty was a middle aged Belgian woman screaming continuously in French (until the morphia took effect). Others soon came – at first civilians and soldiers from our village, then casualties from the battle area just up the road. We soon learned that things were not going well; the village was held by SS Panzer Grenadiers, experienced troops backed by a Tiger tank. This enormous tank outgunned the Shermans easily and set several of them alight; burned and wounded tankmen were amongst our early casualties. The 13th Battalion men had approached the village across the snow-covered fields; the experienced Germans had let them get well out into the open and then opened up with mortar fire which proved devastating on the frozen ground. Many of these who had chatted with us that morning were now dead or severely wounded. The casualties poured in, walking, carried by their friends, slung across jeeps. We had to sort them out, bandage their wounds and pack them into ambulances to go back to the main dressing station. All were injured badly, bleeding and shocked. Most were stoical, grateful for the cigarettes and tea we gave them. Many were severely wounded, shattered and broken limbs, injuries that would probably cripple them for life. It was here that I had my first experience of acute battle breakdown. A stretcher was brought in with a parachutist lying on his face. I went to examine him and found him shaking all over; his eyes were tight shut and he was moaning and whimpering. I said to the stretcher bearers, 'What's this? Where are his wounds?' They replied, 'Oh, he hasn't any. He's got the twitch!' I looked at the casualty card; on it the battalion medical officer had written 'acute battle exhaustion: evacuate'. I tried to speak to him or to comfort him, but got no response, only further shuddering. So I ticked the card and told them to put him on the next ambulance. I still have the record of that night, written on the pages of the French hotel register in Harry Abbott's clear architectural gothic hand. There were 118 of them in 36 hours, all sent back except for a corporal who died slowly in the middle of the cafe floor. By the end, my hands and clothes were stiff with blood and I was dizzy and exhausted. But we had coped.

This was our first major test, and as it turned out, the toughest assignment which we, as a section, had during the two bitter months of winter campaigning that followed. Nowadays the story of the 'Battle of the Bulge' is fully known: how the elite German troops swept amazingly far under the pall of grey snow-laden clouds but were halted when clear skies allowed the allied flyers to destroy their supply lines of petrol, food and ammunition. It had been necessary to throw us so hastily into the battle, but by the time we arrived they were reeling back – though fighting bitterly and skilfully all the way. Many rash parachutists died in brief sharp battles.

As a medical section we advanced into the pathetic villages of the Ardennes, where the people were shattered, starving and frightened. They had thought the war was over for them; then the Germans had come storming back and the SS had wreaked heavy vengeance, executing resisters and deporting most of the men.

My section spent a week in one village. We arrived in the village very soon after the Germans had pulled out; indeed we took over their aid post and a good deal of first aid equipment which was far better than that issued to us! The following morning a young woman came to our door asking if we had a doctor. Summoning Harry to help with translation (he had excellent, if scholarly, French and I had little), we asked what she wanted. She was the village nurse; the Germans had shot the village doctor; many people were sick; would we come and help?

There followed a strange period as I went twice daily to do medical rounds in the village. I saw elderly men and women with ankles grossly swollen from sitting for days in makeshift air raid shelters. I saw children with rheumatic fever. I saw many injured by air raids and accidents. Where we could we gave first aid. We had few drugs and none to spare. In a letter to my mother on 15 January 1945 I wrote:

At present I am in a fairly recently liberated village where there are no doctors. Consequently I have a large civilian practice with whom I struggle as best I can. My French is improving rapidly perforce: luckily many of the medical terms are much the same. I get called for many things from removing German hand grenades to calming a lady who was having a nervous breakdown because her husband had run away with another woman. I have also had a few very serious cases, especially a small boy with cerebrospinal meningitis. I wish I knew some more medicine.

But it seemed that the villagers valued our concern and attention and certainly appreciated the food we gave them. The nurse, Angelique, proved a cheerful charming girl, who after one long drive through the night with a sick child simply proffered, 'Vous dormez avec moi?' – an invitation I was happy to accept. But next day we were ordered out and off to Holland.

There we were billeted for a few weeks near the town of Venlo. The 6th Airborne were put in there to hold the line while other divisions were being rearranged. It was still bitterly cold – 20 and 30 degrees of frost – but there was little fighting. The Dutch people were in a pitiable state; they had been starving and were still very hungry. Their villages had been shattered and they themselves were filthy; all of them were lousy and because of the fear of typhus we spent much of our time spraying DDT, the new wonder delousing drug, into their clothing.

Then we were ordered home on 24 February – by truck across Belgium, by ferry to Harwich and by train back to our billets, seasoned and salted by a brisk spell of battle. Certainly I felt that I had learned a lot, perhaps more than I wanted. All that training had become reality.

DEFEATING THE GERMANS

After a brief spell of leave we came back to our barracks to get ready for the big airborne operation which we believed would end the war. We knew it would come as soon as the weather improved. My section was filled up with new drafts and Staff Sergeant Smart and I began to lick them into shape. Once again we replanned our equipment and its packing. Harry Abbott became the section clerk and Jack Armitage, a recently joined ex-miner, was designated my batman. We went out on training marches and runs, to get fit. For two weeks we were taken out every day in our full kit – steel helmet, 40 pound backpacks and stretchers – and we were made to run up and down ploughed fields in February mud. We wondered why.

We speculated on where we might be sent, and what sort of an operation it would be; a night drop like D-day, when the parachutists were scattered all over northern France, a tidy daytime operation like the Nijmegen bridge, or an ill planned unsupported disaster like Arnhem?

Then, in early March we were told that it was on. We had a brief spell of leave, packed our bags and moved into a sealed transit camp in Essex for our final briefing. At last we heard what we were to do in operation 'Varsity'. We were to assist in the forcing of the Rhine, the last frontier of Germany. We were taken into the briefing tent and shown a sand table model of our dropping zone, an area of pastures and woods, about five miles east of the Rhine near a village called Hamminkeln. The plan showed many gun emplacements, but we were told that the German artillery would be knocked out by the RAF fighter bombers shortly before we dropped at 10 o'clock in the morning. We were also told that many of the pastures were waterlogged from the winter rains. The area was to be saturated with parachutists – two full divisions – our 6th and the American 17th. We were to be the first wave, then the gliders would follow an hour later. It was to be the largest simultaneous airborne drop ever, some 15,000 men.

We were issued with air photos of the dropping zone and marked our rendezvous points. We checked and rechecked our equipment and our kit bags. We sewed compasses, escape maps and fighting knives into our clothing. We wrote 'last letters' to be sent to our families if we did not come back. I began to wonder how I would manage. I felt elated and frightened. I was about to parachute into action into Germany to smash Nazism finally. This was what I had been preparing for for years, intensively for the last year and a half of army service, but psychologically since 1936 when I had committed myself to the fight against Nazism. I was, of course, tense and jumpy, checking in my mind all the things I had to do. I was frightened – not so much of being killed or wounded, but that I might fail through weakness, cowardice or stupidity and let down my section, the unit and myself. And, of course, I wondered how I would manage under fire, in danger. Would I panic and do silly things? Would I be overcome by fear and try to run away? Would I remember to do all the things we had been told? Of course, I was much supported. I had been well trained, as a doctor, as a soldier, as a parachutist. My body had been toughened and hardened. I had seen some action in Belgium and had been under fire. I was well supported, by comrades who had seen plenty of action, Staff Smart, Harry Abbott. I believed that the Operation plan was sound and would probably succeed. but I still wondered whether I would manage.

March 24 was the D-day. The night before, we packed finally and then rose in the dark to go to our aerodrome where Dakota aircraft waited. My section filled one; we drew our parachutes and did up all our kit; jump jackets, kit bags, shell dressings, plasma bottles and, over it all, the parachute harness. When it was all on we could only just waddle to the plane and climb in. We settled in to await take off. I was sitting in the first seat, just opposite the open door, so I had an excellent view of the last minute activity. Our dispatcher, a lean gum chewing American seemed quite blasé about the trip. The pilot, a major, came to have a word with us.

The engines started up and the Dakotas moved off one after another. Soon our plane taxied out, surged up and then circled to join the formation. We set off southward. It was a bright clear sunny morning and all the land was clear below. We passed over the coast – then back over England! We had passed from Essex across the Thames estuary and were now over Kent. We saw Canterbury cathedral shining in the sun and I had a brisk argument with Harry Abbott saying I thought it inferior to Salisbury. Then over Dover, and the white cliffs gleaming in the morning sun. I wondered if I would ever see them again.

By now we were in a massive flight of planes but as we moved deeper into France we passed another armada of Dakotas, each of them towing a glider. There seemed to be hundreds of them. The gliders were tossing up and down in the slipstream and we felt sorry for the glider troops who would be feeling sick and vomiting. Our plane was fairly steady.

We moved on over Belgium and saw an area of recent battle – shell holes and mud and soon the air became murky – the artillery barrage before the battle; we could see little. Then the first warning 'Stand to the doors' came, we stood up and hooked up our parachutes and shuffled into line. I shuffled up to the door, put my left foot at the open edge of the door and grasped the door frame. 'Red light! Four minutes to go'. Then I saw the Rhine through the murk – a big grey river. Then wooded hills and suddenly bangs and cracks – anti aircraft fire! I heard a rattling sound as shell splinters hit the plane. I saw a Dakota rushing back to safety, flames pouring from its engine. 'Green light! go!' and I plunged out through the door.

There was the usual buffeting from the slip stream and then I swung free and looked around. The land looked familiar. To the north I saw the autobahn as in the air photo and then I was down with a bump. I hit the quick release and let the parachute go, pulled in my kit bag, undid it and put on my rucksack; I was ready to go. It had been just like any jump – yet it was different. The air was murky with gun smoke. There was a continuous row of small arms fire, the whine of bullets, the rattle of machine guns, the thump and crack of heavy guns and the explosions of mortars. It all sounded very dangerous. I decided I had better hurry to my rendezvous and I started for the nearest wood.

I wanted to run, but could not for the ground was soggy, and my pack was heavy and I was soon sweating profusely as I plodded along. I got into the wood to find many paratroopers milling around, no one quite sure where we were. Then Colonel Hewlings appeared and told us where we were – in the wrong wood! We had to go out into the dangerous open fields again! In the wood it seemed safer, though the gunfire was still going on ferociously. By now there were a number of men from our field ambulance, so I called on them to follow me and set off through the wood.

Suddenly I was knocked over by a heavy blow on my belly. I had been shot. A belly wound, probably fatal. Then I realised I did not feel as bad as I should. I moved and felt no pain. I looked at my waist and saw a smoking hole in my belt. I opened my clothing – no wound. I looked up and saw the group of men looking at me in dismay – they had just seen an officer shot down before their eyes! So I grinned at them, got up and we set off again. It was not until two days later, when I took off my clothes, and a ragged piece of shrapnel about the size of a sugar cube dropped out of my trousers, that I realised what happened. It had gone through my equipment and clothing but had then been too spent to penetrate my skin. Only a little more velocity and I would have been dead.

Crossing the fields was frightening. We were ankle deep in water and bullets were flying past us. Several men were lost. Some lay down to seek cover but I decided to push on. I passed various friends, including the sergeant major. Suddenly there was a whoosh! and a glider, as big as a bus, swept softly over my head and plumped down quite near. Immediately the German guns turned on it, and in a few minutes it was ablaze. But by now I was into the wood, at my rendezvous point with 12 Battalion. The wood was full of parachutists, finding their officers and digging in, for the enemy fire was furious. I knew I had to start an aid post. I hung a Red Cross flag on a bush and started treating the wounded who soon came to me, some slight, but many grievous. The next hour was hectic and frightening. Staff Smart joined me, but then suddenly asked for help and I saw he had a severe thigh wound. Harry Abbott and I managed to stem the pulsing arterial blood and bandage him, but he was clearly out of action. Gradually the German firing quietened. Leaving the wounded in care of the orderlies, I pressed on to my next rendezvous, a farmhouse that was to be the battalion aid post. The German farmer's family were sitting dazedly watching as wounded men, English, Americans, Germans, filled all their rooms, their sties and their yard. I moved amongst them, sorting them out, adjusting dressings and setting splints. Tommy Wilson, the Battalion MO, came up and took over from me and I set off with Armitage to the manor house which was to be the field dressing station of the field ambulance.

The firing had stopped and we were out of immediate personal danger. It was a lovely bright morning and I heard a lark singing. All the fields were strewn with parachutists, wrecked gliders and bodies of men and of cattle. I felt a great reaction; I had survived my first day in battle. But there was lots more work to do. When we arrived at the manor house the unit was beginning to function; the surgeons Peter and Johnnie had started operating and I took over my appointed post in charge of the resuscitation room, preparing the severely wounded for their operations. The next twenty four hours are a blur of demanding, exhausting, medical work, transfusing, bandaging, estimating degrees of shock. Many of the wounded did well, but quite a few died and were carried out to the mounting heap in the field outside. I slept and toiled again. Gradually things slackened; there was time to go outside. All the barns were filled with wounded. I found Staff Smart on a stretcher amongst them, weak but stoical and grateful. I heard that several of the section were dead, including Ivor Shobbrook, my excellent corporal, and also one of our doctors, Gordon Sheill.

The fighting had moved away, though there was still gunfire in the distance. Gradually the area was being cleared up and organised. The padre had groups of German prisoners clearing bodies and digging graves. During the second day the ground forces broke through. At first some tanks, rushing ahead, then infantry plodding along and then, to our delight, ambulances to remove our wounded and take over our work. We had a chance to rest, recover and reform. We had done our allotted task – we had landed behind the enemy front line, broken his resistance and held our area until we were relieved. It had not been another Arnhem.

But we had paid a heavy price. The units in the gliders had many killed. Our parachute brigade and our field ambulance had lost a lot of men. I had started out in the plane with a staff sergeant, a corporal, two lance corporals and fifteen men. By the end of the day the corporal and two men were dead, the staff sergeant and one lance corporal and two other men wounded – the section was halved. We needed time to rest and rearrange.

The unit left the manor house and moved into a house in Hamminkeln. Reinforcements joined us. A new staff sergeant and corporal were posted to my section and we began to put our equipment together again and to get to know one another.

We also began to learn about our new position as a conquering army. Up till now, in France, Belgium and Holland we had been liberators – welcomed, providing medical (and other) services for the villages we were in, making happy friendships. Now we were among the Germans, our enemies.

The flat fields, the solid farm houses, seemed very like Holland and Belgium. The main difference was the plump prosperity, fields full of cows, barns full of corn, cellars full of preserves, hams and sausages, well fed women and children, in marked contrast to the starved Dutch and Belgians we had seen only two months earlier.

We were wary of the Germans. They were our enemies. We had heard that they might mount a resistance and try to kill us. The army command, fearful that our morale might be undermined, had issued 'non fraternization' orders. We were not to talk to the Germans, except on official business; we were not to share buildings with them; we were certainly not to socialise with them. We were all a bit uncertain how to proceed; some of the men hated all Germans and wanted to plunder and humiliate them; others were hungry for friendship. Each of us had to work out own attitudes and rationalisation.

The Germans' attitude to us, their conquerors, was not what we expected. They showed very little resentment or hostility. Some scowled but many smiled. All were deferential and keen to obey orders; many wished to be cooperative. All seemed delighted that 'for us the war is over'. The soldiers we captured on the battle-

52

fields turned willingly to necessary tasks such as digging graves and clearing rubbish. The villagers asked for orders and directions. Most of them seemed to welcome authority.

At first, as an earnest and conscientious officer, I disapproved of looting and tried to behave correctly to the Germans, while upholding the non-fraternisation orders. As I was one of the few people in the unit who spoke German, and the only officer who did, I was often called on to interpret, which led to strange encounters.

One day in Hamminkeln the colonel saw two nuns coming up to our house. 'What's that? Two Hun nuns! I don't want anything to do with them! What on earth do they want?' he said 'Go and see them, David, and tell them to bugger off!' So I went to see them. 'Was I the town mayor?' (Well, not really) 'Could I give permission?' (What for?) 'Is it allowed to kill the pig?' At this odd request I felt I had to find out more; gradually the story emerged. They ran an orphanage in the village and food was getting short. They had spent all winter fattening a pig and now wanted to kill it to feed the orphans. Nazi government regulations said that they had to have a permit before a pig was killed and that half the pig had to go to the authorities. They had been to the Town Hall but there was no one there. So now they were looking for the new authorities, and would the Herr Hauptmann please authorize them and where should they bring his half of the pig? I thought of going to the colonel, of sending them further, but then told them that they had my full personal authority to kill the pig and to feed all of it to the orphans. They thanked me profusely and departed promising to remember me in their prayers.

New orders came for us, the unit and the 6th Airborne Division. Since we were fresh and lively the army command had decided to use the parachutists to spearhead the drive across northern Germany. The field ambulance sections were to follow the spearhead troops treating casualties as they arose. Thus began a hectic amazing month in which we swept from the Rhine to the Baltic.

The fighting paratroops at first went forward on foot but gradually acquired all sorts of transport from the Germans, from Mercedes staff cars to farm carts, and even a fire engine. Our unit had a few British army ambulances, but never enough. So part of the time we would be sitting in a German village, sorting out our kit and resting and then the section would be ordered forward in support of the lead battalion. We would pack into ambulances, go forward until the casualties mounted, then set up the aid post in a building (usually a tavern) and start sending the casualties back – a wild and scrappy programme. Sometimes resistance was fierce, sometimes very slight. In some areas the advance was rapid and uncontested. In the villages sheets hung out of the windows in token of surrender; bridges were left open and undamaged; elderly men in uniform – support troops – and anti-aircraft gunners queued up to surrender.

In others sudden fierce resistance flared up. We had just settled into one building when we were suddenly overwhelmed with casualties; severely wounded and shattered parachutists, civilians and a number of very young German air force men. We discovered that they were cadet officers in a fliers' training school, keen, brave, selected elite. Their officers had led them out to kill the invaders and to die for the Fatherland – and they had obeyed, effectively and dangerously.

Another day we drove for 40 miles through sunny farmlands just south of a great lake (the Steinhuder See) and saw hardly any fighting. We set up our aid post in a tavern with the beer still on tap which we passed out to our friends as they marched through the village. Later we settled to an excellent supper of fresh bread and butter, sausage, ham and eggs and fine Rhine wines (a marked contrast to our routine bully beef and biscuits). But soon the casualties started coming in, and we worked all night, dressing them and sending them back down the line.

But it was all dangerous. We lost several comrades in small battles. One of my ambulances missed the route back and went down a side road and was ambushed by some *Volksturm,* (Home Guards) with a *panzerfaust* (bazooka). They set the ambulance on fire killing an orderly and all the wounded inside, who were mostly Germans whom we had treated. Several of our friends who had been posted out to the battalions were shot as they tried to bring in wounded, including a cheerful sergeant who had a Military Medal for his bravery in the retreat from Burma.

Armitage, my batman, was an odd character, very talkative. Rather older than the others, he had been a Red Cross man down the mines and told many tales of the injuries he had seen. In the dressing stations he was quite useful, if too garrulous; I noticed that the other men had not much use for him. I was somewhat surprised one day to hear his account of how we went into action on 24 March. It was far more colourful than my recollection including the statement that he saw a piece of shrapnel the size of his fist pass between my legs as I stood to the door of the aircraft! One morning, four weeks into Germany, Ray Kirkham, who was working as unit medical officer, told me that he was going to send Armitage 'down the line'; at sick parade that morning he had sobbed and said he could take no more. Armitage confirmed this: 'I can't stand no more, sir, I really can't; I'm too old for this sort of thing. I'm sorry, sir, but I've got to go'. He collected his kit and got on the next ambulance and we never saw him again.

On one occasion when were closely following the front troops I took a wrong turning, and found myself in advance of the fighting! We were driving through a burning village when I saw German soldiers running out with white flags to surrender. We were the first British soldiers they had seen. We scuttled back quickly to the nearest British troops!

We passed through villages and small towns but bypassed the big towns on our route, like Wesel, Munster, Osnabruck, Minden and Hanover for they had all been devastated by bombing. As we moved across the North German plain, fertile and prosperous and beautiful, we began to become aware of what life had been like in wartime Germany. The German civilians in the countryside were well fed and plump but weary of the long sad war, glad it was over but fearful of the future. Most of the German soldiers were glad to have a chance to surrender, and told tales of fanatical officers insisting on pointless last ditch battles. But what amazed us were all the other nationalities. Cheering us along the roads were people from all over Europe – crowds of French POWs from 1940 wearing remnants of uniform and waving tricolors; sturdy Polish men and women who had been working for the farmers; British and American POWs from recent campaigns, cheerful and fit, but lean and hungry; saddest of all, the Russians, gaunt scarecrows, weak and starved, clothed in rags. A letter written to my mother on 6 April gives my reaction at that time:

55

We are now well into Germany as conquerors – a most interesting business. One rushes along roads in great bounds of tens of miles while down them come two processions – often intermingled. German prisoners sometimes escorted, often walking back to captivity quite unaccompanied, and jubilant Poles, Russians, French, Dutch, Belgians, Greeks, Yugoslavs, Italians. It is an astounding sight. The German people have failed entirely to rally to the defence of their homes. There has not been a vestige of scorched earth. In many places the *Volksturm* rifles and *panzerfausts* are lying neatly stacked in the local police station. Such resistance as there is – at times quite brisk – comes from units of regular soldiers, air force ground troops, static battery gunners, and so on. Occasionally little Hitler Youths give trouble. Most of the Germans are servile in the extreme. I shall never again listen to anyone who speaks of the Germans being a proud race. The civilians are of course frightened of us – they expect murder, fire, rape, arson, loot – but they fawn and cringe far beyond that. One might expect a stiff reserve, a sullen hatred but no – they come out with things. You ask for eggs, milk, hams, guns, cameras – they fall over themselves to bring them to you. I have frequently asked the way and they have been most helpful and co-operative in directing us – no attempt to misdirect us. Never an attempt to retreat into the difficulties of language and confuse us. Extravagant praise for the excellence of my German and polite enquiries as to where I learned it.

In most towns and many villages we would find small stockades of wooden huts surrounded with barbed wire where the Russian prisoners had been kept in filth and starvation. Occasionally we found people in these camps, dying of starvation, amongst all the plump plenty of the German farms. When we spoke to the Germans about it they first said, 'Ah, those Russians, they were just animals, so dirty and barbaric', but then when we protested further, 'Ah well, it was a police and party matter; it was not wise to ask questions'. Few of them seemed ashamed of what had been happening in their own village.

Gradually our attitudes towards the Germans began to harden.

56

But it was the discovery of the concentration camp at Belsen that made the critical change. Our unit was resting near Celle when the news broke. First we heard rumours, then medical reports; the director of airborne medical services had seen the place and had refused to use his parachute field ambulances to clear it out. Typhus was raging; he put a cordon round the camp and flew in special units. In Celle there were many concentration camp prisoners who had been trapped in a train in the station by RAF bombing. We saw the wrecked carriages and the pile of tumbled bodies machine-gunned down by the SS as they tried to flee. We visited the town hospital where many were now being treated. In their prison pyjamas, they were so gaunt that they looked like skeletons, with great deep dark eyes glowing out of the eye sockets in their skull-like faces. They chattered to us – in French, German, English, Polish, Russian, of their delight in surviving. I spoke to one Russian to cheer him up and clapped him on the back; he was so weak he fell on his face.

Then the newsreels of the horrors in Belsen, the mounds of starved dead, the crawling dying, and the sullen brutal SS guards were shown to all the British troops and attitudes towards the Germans changed markedly. This showed particularly in our changing pattern of looting. At first we had been proper in our behaviour. We took from German soldiers their guns and their equipment. We took from the civilians at first only what we needed to fight better – food, eggs, butter, bread, milk, vehicles for travelling, useful articles of clothing. Everyone wanted to have a Luger pistol, the best handgun in Europe and soon most officers had one. Many paratroops equipped themselves with Schmeisser machine pistols, which were far more efficient than our Sten guns. My section acquired several sets of German stretcher bearer scissors, far better than our issue ones. But then our behaviour changed. We began to take watches, binoculars, cameras, from soldiers and then from civilians. Then we began to take things from houses we commandeered; books, clothes, jewellery, if we could find it. Former slave servants would sidle up to us and show us where the family had hidden their black market food or their furs or buried their silver. Some of us were more willing to steal than others. Some boasted openly of how many watches they had stolen. Others limited themselves to official equipment. But after Belsen, restraint vanished. Officers stopped checking looting. The only thing that limited the looting was weight; we had to carry everything we took.

Traditionally, conquering armies have sacked, looted and raped. The 6th airborne Division developed a taste for the first two, but the third was not necessary. The countryside was full of well fed young women with children whose husbands on the Russian front had not been heard of or seen for many months. They were very willing to entertain a British soldier, especially if he brought precious goods like cigarettes or chocolate. However, no German women felt any urge to tempt me and I had no time to develop a liaison.

By Celle we were most of the way across Germany. The war was clearly coming to an end. The Russians were closing in on Berlin. But still there was talk of a last stand in the Alpine redoubt. It was said that the Nazi leaders were going to fall back on the Austrian mountains and hold out there. Ahead of us lay the Elbe – one of Germany's great rivers. The 6th Airborne Division was withdrawn into rest camps; our Unit was in camp near Luneburg. It was said that there would be another parachute operation for us – to force the Elbe, the last barrier. We were dismayed; with the war nearly ended we did not want the danger and deaths of another parachute operation.

Then we heard that it was off. The Elbe had been bridged by the commandos. The paratroopers, however, were to make the last push, and 225 were to support the front brigade. Thus began my last active days of war – an amazing experience. Rising early we surged down to the Elbe and crossed on a Bailey bridge and started the headlong rush for the Baltic. Our ambulances were in a long line of British army vehicles pushing steadily north. Down the other side of the road moved an endless column of German soldiers walking thankfully towards British imprisonment, away from the dreaded Russians. Every unit of the German army was there – field grey jackets, airforce blue, black tank overalls, fit young men, bandaged limping old men with WWI medal ribbons, women auxiliaries in shapeless grey uniforms, even an SS colonel striding along in his black overcoat – an endless stream. They had thrown away their guns and their helmets but still carried their packs as they sought Western captivity.

That night we stopped in a farm a few miles from the Baltic, and still the prisoners poured in seeking someone to whom to surrender. One sergeant major sought our Red Cross unit; he wanted to surrender several hundred men, but also had two perforated ulcers and three gastric crises. I was surprised at his medical jargon; I found that this had been one of the 'gastric ulcer' battalions, formed entirely of men with peptic ulcers!

We were told that there would be a 'cordon sanitaire' established between us and the Russians some ten miles wide. All units were told to keep away from direct contact with Russians. This was too much for me. I found one of our drivers who shared my curiosity and we slipped away from the unit and drove east. We passed through several German villages with sheets hanging from the windows and at last in one of them found some real Russians – three officers and a driver in a commandeered German staff car. We stopped, shook hands, kissed and pounded each other's backs. But communication was difficult; I had no Russian, they no English. But a shabby little man emerged from the crowd that had gathered and offered to translate. I felt that the occasion called for appropriate words, so I declared in broken German: 'Tell my friend that this meeting gives me great joy. It means the final defeat of Hitlerite fascism. It is a great victory for the freedom loving peoples of the world'. I thought it rather good and the little man struggled hard with it. The senior Russian officer, a bespectacled major, unshaven with a bandage round his head, answered briefly. I was told: 'The Major say, Yes. It is good. Now war is over and we can all go home!'

A day later we moved to Wismar, a small port on the Baltic and were told we would now stop. We had reached the Baltic and our war was over! Three days later on 8 May came the news of the official surrender. That evening we fired off all the rockets and tracer in town in a wonderful firework display. In every unit there were wild drunken parties on looted German wine. The war was over and we had survived. I felt amazed, delighted and exhausted, for I had always expected that I would die before the war ended.

However, for the medical services there was still plenty to do.

In Wismar there was a large well equipped hospital, built for the Luftwaffe. 225 Field Ambulance took it over. It was empty when we arrived, but next day several hospital trains steamed in from the east, packed with wounded, doctors, nurses and refugees of every kind. Many of the wounded were in a pitiable state; they had major wounds dressed with paper bandages and they had been lying for days on stretchers in their own pus and faeces. We organised the nurses to get them out and into the wards, to get them cleaned and fed. Our surgeons started operating on the urgent cases. Soon we had a fine hospital running well. I was put in charge of a convalescent ward, containing Germans from the eastern front, airborne wounded and some Russians.

We had started to meet our 'Gallant Russian Allies', the soldiers of the Red Army, and this was a shock for many of us. Roaming the streets of Wismar were Russians with tommy guns, festooned with watches and outrageously drunk, shooting at anything that caught their eyes. Everyday German women came into the clinics saying they had been raped repeatedly by Russians. In my ward I had a Russian sergeant who had been shot in the leg and was having considerable pain. Every morning he would beg me, *'Tovarisch doctor, schiesse mich, schiesse mich!'* (Comrade doctor, shoot me, shoot me). I tried to reassure him but he still begged to be shot.Then one day two dour Russian military policemen came and removed him, to what fate I could not guess.

But we had other, more pleasant contacts with the Russians. Two Russian military surgeons came to visit us, to see their wounded. We gave them lunch in the officers' mess afterward and it turned into a merry affair, despite an almost complete lack of any common language. There were many toasts. To Churchill! To Truman! To Stalin! Then they offered to sing, and the handsome doctor with long silky blonde moustache sang in a beautiful voice several moving songs (apparently about the girls at home). Then he called on us to sing – a request that completely dismayed our group of typical English doctors. However, our dentist, a cheerful lecherous rogue, saved our faces by leading us in the well known song, 'The Bloody Great Wheel' which is set to the sonorous tune of 'All People that on Earth do Dwell' and pleased the Russians who thought it was a patriotic song.

We also had a special divisional concert. Marshal Rokossovsky sent his army concert party to entertain us. The opera house in Wismar was filled with paratroopers. The concert party were all fighting soldiers, but brilliant performers. There were of course massed male voice choirs, singing rousing songs of the Red Army and also Cossack dancers and sword dancers, but best of all were girls dancing the national dances of many Russian races. Most popular was a dark eyed Uzbeck beauty who danced a variant of the dance of seven veils – to tumultuous applause. We were told she was a corporal telephone operator!

After a day or two in the hospital I was detached and told to start a first aid room at the transit camp that had been set up in Wismar. To this camp in a commandeered housing estate were sent all the human flotsam passing through the town – Russians going east, Americans (captured flyers) going west, Frenchmen going west, Poles wondering where to go, Yugoslavs wanting to go south – some cheerfully going home and others anxiously wondering what on earth the new Europe would have for them. I had to treat their illnesses, if I could, and help them on their way. I had medical supplies (including lots of disinfecting powder) and medical orderlies, but major comprehension difficulties. I recruited a Latvian lawyer with many languages and his daughter as my interpreters and did the best I could. I soon learned *'boleh'* (pain) and *'ochen boleh'* (much pain), but complex diagnosis was impossible. However, I heard all sorts of amazing personal stories and met many people who had found a fair life under Hitler's new order and were very frightened of the freedom we thought we were bringing them. I had much to think on as a letter to my mother on 11 May reveals:

Well the war is over here. To me it doesn't seem to mean so very much, though I suppose it must be wonderful to all of you at home.

We had a hectic dash to the Baltic, and for 24 hours Germans surrendered in thousands. Then the Russians came. Since then I have worked in a vast hospital looking after German wounded evacuated from the Russians. I am now in medical charge of a camp of refugees of one sort and another. Lots of work to do.

Escaped POWs of all sorts come through telling of what is going on behind the Russian lines. Pitiful wretches show up from German concentration camps. Russians go through on their way back home.

I am very oppressed by the amount of beastliness about – of man to man of all sorts. I am sick of tales of rape of all sorts and kinds, of beatings and of starvings, of murders and slaughter. Beside all these things battlefields seem fine and clean and honourable. I see the Dragon's Teeth being sowed everywhere and the shape of the next war looming clear. In fact, I am depressed.

Otherwise I am healthy, even though antilouse powder exudes in continuous showers from my clothing!

However, I persevered with helping my refugees. I bullied army quartermasters and German bureaucrats and got food, clothes and necessaries. But this did not last long. The army command wanted the paratroops back in England and we were warned to depart. My refugees gave a magnificent farewell party, which ended with fifteen burly Russians tossing me in the air – an alarming experience but apparently a traditional Russian way of showing appreciation. Packing to return presented a problem to us because of all we had acquired. We were told that we could only take what we could carry so there was much discarding of treasured items. So finally, deeply laden with loot, we staggered into the aircraft and flew back home to England, our billets and our victory leave.

PREPARING FOR BATTLE 1943/4

Just got my wings! Mother's favourite photograph

Ready for a parachute jump

On leave with Mary Rose

EUROPE 1945

January 1945. Staff Sergeant Smart at our first Belgian dressing station

April 1945. With my section in Germany

May 1945. Wismar. Meeting the Russians

SUMATRA 1945

Langley

16 September 1945. Lady Louis inspects the Bangkinang internment camp

PALESTINE 1946

Medical staff, psychiatric wing, 12 British General Hospital, Sarafand. Author (second from left), Manugian, McCombe, Blair

The Warrior Returns! Marriage October 1946

TO THE EAST

So we came home to England in May, elated and victorious. It was a lovely summer and everyone was delighted that the European war was over. The blackout was finished, the street lights were on once again, we could drive with blazing headlights. There was a great sense of freedom and delight. Soldiers were coming home from Europe and the papers were full of the speeches of the politicians preparing for the election soon to be held.

But for some of us and for me personally there was a shadow. The war in the Far East was still going on. As 225 and 6th Airborne came back to England, we were split into two groups. The 'old soldiers', those who had been in the army since the early days of the war, and would soon be for demobilisation, who had done their bit and would not be expected to go east, and the recently conscripted like myself who would be. We were told that the armies in India desperately needed experienced fighters and trained parachutists. We were warned that we would be for tropical service as soon as possible; then we were given four weeks leave – two weeks disembarkation leave as returned warriors and two weeks embarkation leave for the Far East!

I hurried up to London to see Mary Rose and to ask her to get some holiday, and then up to Edinburgh to tell my mother the tales of how I (and others) had defeated Nazism. We chatted for many hours and listened to the election speeches on the radio. This was the first election in which I would have a vote and I would, of course, vote for the Labour Party. I was saddened to hear Churchill ranting wildly and predicting that Harold Laski would introduce a Gestapo if Labour were elected. I realised that his rhetoric was immensely heartening if one agreed with him – as I had done in 1940 – but just rather silly when he was wrong.

Then south to collect Mary Rose and go down to Devon. My brother, Ralph, who was at the Royal Marine Training School at Thirlestane in south Devon, had found us lodgings in a part of the south Devon coast which had been out of bounds for five years. We had a delightful fortnight there which was in effect our honeymoon; long days together walking the cliffs and beaches, making love at night, getting to know each other properly. We felt truly and permanently committed and discussed marriage. We decided that there was little point as I was to go off to the Far East so very soon. Though I did not tell this to Mary Rose, I knew that parachute assaults on Japanese positions would be deadly; I was convinced that I personally would not survive another parachute operation. I also had a deeper certainty – dating from 1939 – that like Denys Barnes and Peter Cheyne I was doomed to die in this war. So marriage seemed pointless. But we had a lovely time together and we discussed the world after the war and how socialism would ensure a just and fair society.

Then I went back to Longford where I found 225 being split apart. Many old friends, like Harry Abbott, had been posted away because of their impending demobilisation. New members were being posted in, including men from the medical units of First Airborne who had survived Arnhem and got back later after months of hiding with the Dutch underground. It was a new, uneasy, gathering. Except for the regulars, most of us were resentful at being sent to further danger, fearful of the Japanese, of being killed, of suffering tropical diseases and of being away from England and our families for many years.

Soon came orders. 5 Parachute Brigade was to go out to India as soon as possible. Advance parties from all units were to go forthwith. The advance party of 225 Parachute Field Ambulance would be headed by Captain D.H. Clark! We were to leave in a few days. We were all issued with 'tropical kit'. This was not, as we had expected, khaki shorts and pith helmets, but strange dark green stuff, curious shaped equipment and boots with rubber soles. This we were told was the latest jungle equipment, lightweight and camouflaged.

I phoned Mary Rose and she came down to Longford for one last weekend of frenzied lovemaking. I saw her off at Salisbury station and I long remembered how her face disappeared as the train swept off round a bend. I felt sure that she would never see me again.

A few days later the advance party assembled and we were put on a train. After many hours wandering across Britain we arrived in Glasgow and were hurried on to a troopship. Later that day we departed. It was not as furtive as our earlier departures to battle – there was even a military band playing for us at the station – but it felt sad and poignant. We went down the Clyde in gathering dusk, and my last sight of my native land was Ailsa Craig.

We soon settled onto the boat. It was crowded, but not too full. I was in a cabin with other parachute medical officers of 5 Brigade, Ian Prentice, Ian Barclay and James Scott. I had not known any of them before, but I got on – in the usual superficial army way – quite well with Ian Prentice, a tall quiet serious man and Ian Barclay, a droll but cheerful man, but I did not care for Scott, an uncouth man who had only recently joined the army and resented in a clumsy ineffectual way everything that happened to him. I realised how much I had learned in two years about how to rub along in the army – not expecting much, not resenting much, never complaining, never answering back. We tried to tell him, but he would not learn, and so found himself constantly landed with the unpleasant duties such as orderly officer and the latrine inspections.

We were all allocated tasks in the temporary society of the troopship; I wangled responsibility for the ship's library, a task I found most congenial especially since all work was done by an earnest intelligence corps corporal. Shortly after we started I fell ill and was admitted to the sick bay with appendicitis; the doctors considered operating but decided to try conservative treatment, and I recovered uneventfully.

After a few rough days in the Bay of Biscay we sailed into the Mediterranean, my first time in that famous sea, past Gibraltar and along the coast of Algeria, where veterans of the First Parachute Battalion told us great tales of their legendary deeds in 1942. Then to Suez and through the Canal to Port Said – desert,

65

camels, Bedouin, many fascinating sights.

Life on board was essentially dull. There was not much to do and of course we were not allowed ashore. There were boat drills, physical training and kit inspections. The medical officers were called on to lecture the troops on tropical diseases. I found myself swotting the subjects up from little army handbooks and passing on information and warnings almost certainly incorrect. The only person alarmed was, I think, myself! I came to feel that 'the tropics' were a pullulating festering morass, filled with innumerable insects, reptiles and animals, all carrying foul and fatal diseases and intent on biting and infecting me personally. I was even more convinced I would never see home again.

As we were passing through the torrid Red Sea, the news of the general election came through – a massive landslide victory for the Labour Party! I was delighted, but I had to keep my delight to myself for the officers mess on the ship was unshakably Tory and all the talk that evening was that the country would 'go to the dogs', that England would no longer 'be fit for gentlemen to live in', and that the best thing to do would be to emigrate to one of the 'decent colonies' like South Africa or Australia.

So, on through the Red Sea, when I was hotter than I had ever been before, and across the Indian Ocean to Bombay. Our landing was strange and exotic. Everyone was shouting and all seemed angry. Everywhere fat brown men with lists and papers shouted at lean brown men who were dropping their loads (often our baggage). I remember looking down on the dockside and seeing all that Kipling had prepared me for.

After the confusion which seemed inseparable from any army move, we were put on a train and after a few hours' journey were put off in the dark at a siding, where we were not expected. I was shown a bare concrete walled hut and told to sleep there. No bed, no facilities. Worse, no mosquito net! I had been told these were essential for survival in 'the tropics'. The cell was full of the buzzing, whining and rattling of insects flying at the lamp. When I put it out, I saw them flying around luminescent, still looking for me! I slept little that night.

Next day we found out we were at Kalyan, a vast transit camp outside Bombay where we stayed for two weeks while our senior officers tried to find out what we should do. Soon after our arrival, the monsoon started. Every day it rained, vast downpours and it was steamy hot. We were issued with broad brimmed hats and monsoon capes – shapeless garments that shed much of the downpour – but everything became damp and horrid. I would take off my boots in the evening and find them spotted with furry mould in the morning. The food was horrid, badly prepared English type food and we were soon all complaining vociferously. We were made to go out for marches 'to get fit' and there was much checking of rolls and numbers and kit. The officers' mess for the transit camp was a shabby depressing place full of curious men in a variety of uniforms all waiting for someone to decide where they should go and complaining constantly about their fate.

The only relief was the chance to go into Bombay, a fascinating city, full of colour and smells and an incredible variety of people – big and small, dark brown and light brown, prosperous and desperately poor, all hurrying, all shouting at each other. We made for the Taj Mahal Hotel, which was the main officers' club. A vast rambling building, it stood at the edge of the sea, beside the 'Gateway to India', a triumphal arch in Roman style put up to mark an imperial occasion. We specially favoured the dining room, because it was the only air conditioned room, cool and dry, a delicious feeling. The diners were a fascinating collection, mostly officers, but of many services and races, squat dark brown Gurkha officers, tall turbanned Sikhs, small plump voluble Hindus, but more exciting were the women, particularly the beautiful Parsees, slim, pale skinned and immensely graceful in their glittering saris. How they showed up the few English women officers – pink, fat, clumsy, perspiring!

It was on 16 August in the Taj Mahal that news came through that the war was over! A new bomb had been dropped on Japan and the Japanese had surrendered! We were amazed and delighted. Maybe we would not have to die after all! There was excitement and celebration everywhere. The ships in Bombay harbour put on all their lights and fired off rockets. The hotel was uproarious as we all got drunk and cheered and sang all night. Suddenly we were reprieved! How happy we were! I remember pointing out to Paddy Freeman that I would never have to do another parachute operation, and with any luck not even another jump! At one stage in the celebrations I found myself in a maudlin circle out on the quay by the 'Gateway to India' as we sang 'Bless 'em All', the old troopers' song, with its relevant line, 'They say there's a troopship just leaving Bombay, bound for old Blighty's shore'. As the group, hoarse and weary, broke up I saw that we were being gazed at quietly by a crowd of dispassionate Indians, while behind them the street beggars were settling down for the night on the pavement. They had no interest in the war, nothing to fear from the Japanese, and certainly nothing to celebrate.

We wondered what would happen now that the war was over, but it soon became clear that the army was carrying on regardless. On 19 August we were sent south for jungle training. We were put on a train which rumbled its way across India to Madras. The country was lovely, green and fresh after the monsoon, but sunny. The train was slow, so slow going up hills that one paratrooper jumped off, caught a butterfly in his hat and jumped back on again. From Madras we went through Bangalore to Gudulur training camp and into the jungle to learn 'jungle warfare'. We were issued with machetes and taught about the different kinds of bamboo and how to use them for our survival. It all seemed rather pointless and I wondered how long I should be doing such fatuous things. Some of the officers rejoiced in the prospect of peacetime soldiering in India – 'A gentleman's life, old boy!'; I was appalled at the prospect. The officers' mess began to divide – the majority of temporary soldiers, like myself, talking of when we might be demobilised, and the regulars and those who had opted to stay on in the army trying to maintain 'good order and military discipline' and attempting to maintain the sense of purpose and high morale that had marked the parachute units for the previous four years. I recall one rather fatuous major who harangued us after one particularly exhausting jungle exercise for leaving litter; 'We must leave the jungle tidy' he cried in impotent fury.

INTO ACTION AGAIN

Everyone was irritable and angry, trapped in pointless army games. I felt resentful and even mutinous. Was I going to have to spend months or even years messing about in this seedy country doing pointless army training? The war was over; the Nazis had been defeated, the Japanese had surrendered. I wanted no part in maintaining the out of date structure of the British empire.

Then, suddenly, on 26 August all the paratroop doctors were called to the camp office; we were to go to Ceylon forthwith. We set off and on 28 August, my birthday, I found myself in Bangalore. I went to visit a German couple to whom Gus Born had given me an introduction, Dr and Mrs Brinnitzer. He was an elderly refugee doctor who had come out to India in the thirties and had found congenial work in this pleasant city. I had met them when I passed through earlier. Now they welcomed me and gave a delightful little party, with sophisticated intellectual European guests – a brief moment of civilization amidst the barren philistinism of army life.

When we arrived in Kandy we were addressed by the director of army medical services for India who explained the important task they wanted us for. The surrender had uncovered Japanese prison camps scattered all over South East Asia. A special organisation was being set up to deal with the problem – to find the prisoners, to succour them and to bring them home. It was to be called RAPWI (Repatriation of Allied Prisoners of War and Internees). They badly needed doctors: there were many terrible medical problems. Further, they needed doctors who could be dropped into remote camps. We were the only readily available group of parachute doctors. Would we do it? I was excited and delighted to have something worth while to do – but frightened of yet another jump, after all!

Fired with enthusiasm we set off for our task – only to have it dashed when we found ourselves in a badly run transit camp at Minnirya, full of doctors and others who had been waiting for weeks for the RAPWI assignments. We sat around grumbling for days. Then on 5 September I was sent to Colombo, to the base camp of Force 133, to be kitted out. There we were taken in hand by the staff of Force 133, the clandestine forces who had been infiltrating agents into occupied countries of South East Asia. It was all exciting, exotic, fascinating. We had of course all heard many tales of the strange irregular units that had developed during the war – they were the matter of constant gossip and legend – Popski's Private Army, the Special Air Service, the Special Boat Service, Force 136, Force 133, SOE and others. They were secret and clandestine – you should not ask too much. They were exotic and different; they wore their parachute wings on their chests, while we wore ours on our shoulders. I had occasionally met them in officers' bars where they told great tales and affected to despise us 'ordinary parachutists' who stayed safely (!) in organised units. Once I had even met them in battle. In one battered Ardennes town in January two strange jeeps surged into the village. Their occupants were a wild piratical crew, sporting whiskery beards and moustaches, wearing a variety of uniforms and different coloured hats and berets (green, red and black) and wearing body armour and bullet proof vests. Their jeeps had massive aircraft machine guns mounted fore and aft. After accepting our food and drink and asking a few condescending questions, they had swept off in pursuit of the fleeing Germans. Now I was to join this strange, romantic band!

We spent a few days in a beautiful camp by the warm Ceylon Sea, in tents beneath coconut palms (from which the heavy coconuts would fall alarmingly and unexpectedly). I was equipped with a whole set of new equipment, including valuable objects like binoculars and an excellent Swiss watch. When I prepared to sign for them (as one always had to do in the army) the quartermaster laughed and said they did not bother with that in Force 133 – anything that went on an operation was written off. I was delighted with these new free toys I had acquired, until I realised that in all probability they not only 'wrote off' the equipment, but also the person who carried it!

Then we returned to Minnirya to await our mission. The camp was full of a variety of people; different races, different services, different uniforms, and every day groups would disappear on their missions. None of us knew where we were to go, or when, so the camp was awash with rumours; a group had been dropped into Singapore and were living it up in Raffles, the luxury hotel; a group had been dropped in the sea by accident and all drowned; all the aircraft were obsolete and breaking down and crashing; the parachutes were surplus, condemned American supplies and usually failed to open, and so-on.

Then, one day, mine was amongst the names called over the tannoy to go to the camp office. There I was given my assignment. I was to be the medical officer in Captain Langley's team to go to Bangkinang in Sumatra. Sumatra? Where or what was that? Bangkinang? Where was that? Who was there? What did I have to do?

I met Captain Langley and found he did not know much more. It appeared that following the surrender allied officers had been sent to the various Japanese commands and had been going round assessing the prison camps. As they found them, they radioed out details and the RAPWI teams were assembled, equipped and sent in. Our assignment was a camp in the jungles of Northern Sumatra containing about 6,000 men, women and children, mostly Dutch. They were said to be in a pathetic state. Our task was to get in, assess the situation, take charge, do what was necessary, radio for supplies and await the coming of the relief forces of the British army. Simple! Of course, I was quite accustomed by now, in the army, to being sent off on a task with an inadequate briefing, and doing the best I could when I got there, but I still found the lack of information on this project rather alarming. I remember that all my notes on the operation fitted easily onto the back of an envelope! Langley, however, did not seem bothered. A powerful man of medium height, with the burly build of a rugger player and a battered face, he wore SAS parachute wings, medals for the north African and Italian campaigns, a Royal Scots

71

Fusilier bonnet and a Kukri hanging from his hip. He soon informed me that he too had only recently arrived in India. He had spent 1944 and 1945 with Force 136 in Northern Italy leading groups of partisans during the last bitter winter of war; his group were mostly Italian communists, with a scattering of others, Yugoslavs, escaped Russians and German deserters. He was clearly an experienced warrior, well accustomed to working with a mixed bunch of people on irregular assignments.

He admitted that he knew little of what we had to do. He had known of German POW camps in Italy, but had no experience of Japanese. I told him of my experience of the concentration camps in north Germany a few months earlier; I remember telling him that we would discover appalling and revolting chaos; that our first task would be to separate out those who might live from those who were bound to die or who were already dead, and that emergency doctoring would be the first task of the team.

That evening we met the rest of our hastily assembled team. My medical orderly, Sergeant Atherton, a lean sardonic seasoned man, yellow with antimalarial drugs, came from the RAF. He had had plenty of medical experience, had trained as a parachutist in India and had been working on drops in Burma. The Dutch group was led by Lieutenant Ledeboer, an anxious, pale Dutchman who had fought in the resistance in Holland during the previous winter and had now volunteered to come east to help to recover the Netherlands East Indies. With him was Sergeant van Onselaar, a tall fair Dutchman and Sergeant de Man, a tall brown smiling man, a Dutch Eurasian who had spent the war in Holland. All of them could speak Malay, which was essential. The last member was the wireless operator, a small quiet man named Tan Tjeng En, a Chinese who spoke very little English; he had been a member of Chiang Kai-shek's army and had somehow become part of the British forces.

We tried to gather what information we could about our task. We were told that another RAPWI team, headed by Major Boitteaux of Force 133, with my friend Ian Barclay as medical officer, had been dropped at Pakanbaroe, a town not far from Bangkinang where there was said to be a large camp full of British and Dutch prisoners of war. They had flown off on 8

September and we heard they had landed safely.

On 10 September we gathered before dawn and were taken to China Bay aerodrome and our plane, a Liberator. It was a heavy whale of a plane with its large hold filled with enormous petrol tanks, sufficient to fly across the southern Indian Ocean and back. The six of us were packed in a small space in the tail of the plane; we would exit down a chute. The take-off was difficult; the plane had to taxi for an immense distance before it slowly lifted off and pointed its nose at the rising sun. I wondered whether my adventure would finish there and then in the Ceylon Sea.

The journey was long and uneventful. We munched sandwiches, dozed and I wrote in my diary. Finally, about 1.30 the crew told us we were over Sumatra. Looking down, all I could see was a carpet of dark green treetops. Langley and the first two went out and then I followed with the others. It was a pleasantly high drop and there was time to look around – I saw forest and paddy fields – then I realised I was drifting toward a wide grey river and began to haul on my lift webs and spill round to avoid a ducking.

I made a good and easy landing on a piece of grass beside a paddy field and began to disentangle myself. I saw people coming toward me and suddenly realised that the one in front was carrying a rifle, wearing a sword and was a swarthly oriental. I was terrified! This must be one of these fierce Japanese warriors about to slay me! I began to fumble for my automatic, determined to die bravely. Before I could do anything foolish, however, he halted, stood to attention, saluted smartly and beamed a warm smile. He was in fact a local policeman, delighted to see a returning European. He rapidly called some coolies and ordered them to carry my parachute, my kitbag and my backpack and we set off across the paddies to the road.

To my astonishment, along the road came a British army ambulance – Austin motor, red cross and all. I could not believe my eyes. (I found out later it was Japanese war booty from Singapore 1941). It stopped and out of it emerged a group of white men, all dressed in white shirts and shorts and wearing Red Cross armbands. I could see that they were very thin, but they were also clearly vigorous and effective. Wondering who they were, I said, haltingly, 'Good Day! Is there-anyone-among-you-who-can-speak-English?' A tall distinguished looking grey bearded man stepped forward and said in fluent English, 'Welcome, we are most happy to see you. Allow me to introduce myself – Professor Dr Vaandrager of the East Indian College of Tropical Medicine. May I also introduce my colleagues – Professor Dr Van Meeringen, Professor Dr Van Waardenburg . . .' 15 of them, all professors! I hurriedly revised my vision of pathetic chaos awaiting my brilliant medical skills! Things were clearly going to be rather different.

They took me to the camp headquarters, where the rest of the team were. All had landed safely except for Tan Tjeng En who had fallen into the river but had swum ashore. There were many introductions and Langley and I began to inspect the camps. We soon realised that the position at Bangkinang was quite different from what we had expected. It was clear that the Dutch were well organised and ready for us. They explained that they had been visited a few days earlier by a Major Jacobs, a South African Dutchman of Force 133, who had sent out their details and told them that a team would be coming in soon. They made many introductions – the senior Dutch official of the men's camp Residente Van Brackel and Mevrow Van Brackel, the elected leader of the women's camp, Mevrow Holle, the senior medical officer and many others.

Finally we got started on our tasks. Tan Tjen En tried to get his wireless going, Ledeboer and his group began making contacts in the camps, Langley and I started an inspection. The first thing Langley and I did was to walk round both the camps and assess the situation. The two camps lay to the west of Bangkinang village about two km apart. The men were in a former rubber factory, the women in makeshift barracks. In between was the camp of the Japanese guards. All the camps were ramshackle wood buildings. They had been appallingly overcrowded (970 men, 2,220 women), but now were just over full, as hundreds of internees, especially the younger men and all the sick, had been moved to Padang on the west coast of Sumatra just before we arrived. The men's camp now contained 550 men, many of them blond sunburned Dutchmen, but also brown Eurasians who had been graded as Dutch by the Japanese and interned. Amongst them were a number of former soldiers and policemen. The Japanese had recognised as 'leader' of the camp the senior Dutch official, Resident Van Brackel, a sad tired old man. We learned later that he had been ineffective, supine and unduly co- operative and that he had been much criticised.

The women's camp was larger (1,290 people) but seemed livelier, perhaps because of a number of young children. They were running around naked, or nearly so, deeply sunburned, though some of the very blond Dutch children had never tanned properly so that there were bright pink areas of recurrent peeling on the tips of their shoulders and the ends of their noses. The women were of all ages and colours, but all painfully thin; many of the older women were gaunt and careworn, but some of the younger Dutch and Indonesian girls looked lively and even pretty. Many of them had already made themselves dresses from the parachutes of the Red Cross containers dropped a few days earlier. The leader of the women's camp was Mevrow Holle. Since the Japanese recognised no seniority amongst women, they had allowed them to elect their own leader and we learned how well they had chosen. Mevrow Holle, the wife of a judge, was a courageous woman and she had again and again stood up to the Japanese even though this had earned her repeated beatings.

We were shown the kitchens, the washing areas, the lavatories, the workshops, the kitchen gardens – all in good order. We were taken to a hospital in Bangkinang village to which they had moved the sick from both camps after the surrender. There were only a few people there because many had already been moved. They were clearly being well looked after by Dutch doctors and nursing sisters, though two men were obviously dying. The Dutch doctors discussed with me what they were doing and planned to do for the sick – and I quickly realised that they were all far more skilful doctors than I was. It seemed that there would be no medical role for me here!

The Japanese prison guards were in a camp halfway between the two internment camps. They had withdrawn there after the surrender and had very little contact with their former prisoners. In due course we met the commander, Captain Hashimoto, his officers and his medical officer, Dr Kukubu.

It was clear that the camps were being run well by the Dutch and that there was nothing that the RAPWI team had to do urgently. We, therefore, applied ourselves to communication. Tan Tjeng En got his radio working and we began to send out messages. Langley drafted reports on the state of the camp and its needs, and during the next weeks we arranged a number of aircraft drops of food, drugs and clothing.

We soon made contact with Boitteaux's team at Pakanbaroe. They had an RAF officer attached to them and he quickly reported the airstrip fit for use; allied planes, mostly Dakotas, started flying in with Red Cross supplies and repatriation staff. The problems at Pakanbaroe were very different from those in Bangkinang. The prisoners of war, mostly British, were very weak, severely diseased and many dying; their only desire was to get home. Relief teams were being flown in and evacuation was to start as soon as possible.

I went up to Pakanbaroe (three hours drive) on 13 September and found it very busy. The air strip was active and planes were flying in and out. Many strange characters were bustling about. Because Pakanbaroe was only about 250 km, two hours flying time from Singapore, it was easy to hop on one of the planes coming to pick up the POWs. As a result there were reporters and news photographers rushing around, doctors, nurses, Red Cross workers sorting out the POWs and a number of other people who, it seemed, had just come for a trip. Amongst them I met Bob Blair, the airborne corps psychiatrist, plump and sweating under his red beret. He greeted me jovially and told me that my comrades of 225 Parachute Field Ambulance were now in Singapore.

I met the English prisoners of war who had been working on the building of a railroad, and the Dutch doctors who had been trying to provide medical services. Conditions had been appalling; all were starved and horribly lean; everyone had malaria giving them frequent bouts of fever; most had beri beri which made their ankles swollen, pellagra causing diarrhoea and many had tropical ulcers festering on their shins. The doctors had been allowed no drugs and no bandages but they had kept their morale and medical interest. They took me round their hospital, they demonstrated a post mortem and showed me a microscope they had made out of field glass lenses and bamboo. I was deeply impressed. They all told tales of Japanese brutality, beatings, humiliations, executions and sadistic torturing. They said that the Korean guards were the most cruel.

The emaciated English POWs sat on the ground in apathetic groups awaiting their turn to emplane. They were eager to talk to anyone who could tell them of home and since I had left England only six weeks before I was much in demand. They were eager for news, any news, but particularly news of home. How bad had the bombing been? How was life in England now? What did people think of them and their surrender in Singapore in 1941? I informed and reassured them all I could, but it was not always easy.

Amongst the figures strutting around the airstrip was a buxom English woman in khaki shirt and shorts, with a revolver on one side of her belt and a machete on the other. She wore the insignia of an RAF officer and a chestful of medals (I learned later that she was an SOE operative, who had served with SOE and Force 136 in France with distinction and gallantry). But she was a strange sight and one of the ex-POWs asked me, 'Gorblimey, sir, is that what women are like in England now?' I wondered what they would make of the life that had developed during the last five years since they last saw England in 1940.

In our early days in Sumatra there was considerable administrative confusion. Messages and orders came through intermittently; senior officials; British officers, including a medical general, and Dutch civilians flew in to make assessments and give promises and assurances and then disappeared without trace. Plans were constantly changed. We had performed our primary task at Bangkinang. We had assessed the situation and ensured the welfare of the internees; food was coming regularly to the camp and supplies were being dropped frequently. At Pakanbaroe the evacuation was proceeding rapidly and the British prisoners of war would be gone sòon. But where were the Dutch to go?

Langley, now a major, became very active, flying to Singapore to consult with SEAC headquarters, driving over to Padang where a brigade of 26 Indian Division had landed and bustling up to the Japanese army headquarters at Bukit Tingi to discover what the policy was to be and to demand transport, money, facilities for our work.

He told me to remain at Bangkinang and maintain the British presence there. Atherton stayed with me, managing medical liaison with the internees' excellent medical service.

Ledeboer and his group went to Pakanbaroe and then disappeared on some clandestine Dutch undercover operation. To replace them came a group of Dutch RAPWI workers, members of the KDP (Kantoor Displaced Persons) the Dutch refugee organisation. They worked with me for the next month, Sergeant Braskamp and Sergeant Eetje Klinkhamer, a brisk Argentinian Dutch girl who enlivened our little group at Bangkinang with her guitar playing of Dutch and American folk songs. Their task was to arrange and manage the transfer of internees to Padang.

BANGKINANG

I began to take stock of where I was and the perplexing land I was in. Sumatra, a big island 1,700 km long and 400 km wide, had been one of the jewels of the Netherlands East Indies, rich and fertile, with vital oil wells in the south. The part we were in, however, was an area of no value to anyone, a vast low lying jungle of swamps and forest, some 300 km wide, most of it uninhabitable. There were sluggish rivers winding through and a scattering of small villages and towns along them. Pakanbaroe, a little inland port, 100 km from the sea, lay across from Malacca in Malaysia. From it a road ran south, through the jungle, then up the mountains to Bukit Tingi (Fort de Kok) and then down to the western sea coast at Padang, a major seaport and the capital of central Sumatra. Bangkinang was a village on this road, 60 km from Pakanbaroe but still in the lowlands. It lay 30 km from the equator, 150 km from the sea and 20 m above sea level. It was thus hot and humid by day and night.

In a rubber plantation near this dreary village, the Japanese had built two internment camps and put in them the Dutch and Eurasian civilians from central Sumatra. They held them there for three years, on very short rations. They did not, however, make them do forced labour and they allowed them to maintain reasonable order and hygiene in the camps. The camps contained many Dutch administrators and senior Dutch doctors; they controlled disease and infections effectively. They had checked mosquitoes and there was no malaria. They had maintained strict hygiene and boiled all water and there was no dysentery. They had made vitamin extracts and controlled deficiency diseases. However, during the last year, the long term effects of three years' malnutrition had

79

begun to show and older people started to die of beri beri and hunger oedema. In the three weeks since the surrender, the Japanese had provided adequate food, fresh meat and fresh vegetables, and allied planes had dropped considerable medical supplies so that general health was improving. Acute hunger was satisfied and the sick were being treated. However, everyone was thin, feeble and apathetic and all were fearful of the future.

In 1944 the Japanese had attempted to build a railway across Sumatra southward from Pakanbaroe and had brought a large number of British POWs across from Malaysia to construct it. Their conditions had been appalling and many had died. After the surrender they had all been brought back to Pakanbaroe.

Pakanbaroe was a small town, Bangkinang a village, both deep in endless jungle. Both had always been at the back of beyond despite Japanese attempts to develop the port of Pakanbaroe. All buildings were of wood and roofed with palm thatch. The locals were small, dark, handsome people, lean and lively, talking Malay, though everywhere were Chinese traders and merchants. Around the villages and alongside the river were cultivated fields and paddy fields but they were not extensive. There were a few plantations, of rubber and pineapples, but these had not been a success and the Japanese had let them run down. It was much what I had been prepared for by reading Conrad and Maugham but I found the climate far more debilitating than I had expected. We were just on the equator and the sun's heat at midday was devastating. I wore a broad brimmed hat all the time but even then the reflected glare would make my eyes weep. I could do nothing at midday except lie sweating on my bed. I sweated by day, I sweated by night. Whatever I did I sweated and soaked my clothing. It was never cool and I soon developed 'prickly heat', an itching prickling rash all over my body which kept me in constant discomfort.

However, there were compensations about life in Bangkinang. Just opposite the main camp stood the bungalow where the manager of the rubber plantation had lived. We decided to make this our base and it was home for myself, Atherton and our team for the next two months. It was a pleasant roomy building, set in a grove of rubber trees. There was a wide verandah which was our dining room and office and a number of bedrooms. Behind were servant quarters where some trained Malay servants soon appeared to care for our every need. Whenever I approached the bungalow the number one boy, Amat Toka, would appear to greet me and put a glass of freshly pressed lime juice in my hand. I would go into my room and strip off my sweat-sodden clothes. They were at once removed and washed and ironed and would be back an hour or so later. Delightful meals were available whenever we wanted them (or our diarrhoea allowed us to eat). The place was kept spotlessly clean despite the many insects that flew and crawled around us, especially in the evenings. We had a small radio and could listen to the allied forces broadcasts. We had a constant flow of visitors. Allied staff of many kinds came posting up the road: RAPWI officers, St John's and Red Cross administrators, obscure figures from SOE and Force 133, even the allied war graves commission! They came in a wide variety of uniforms and with an extraordinary range of excuses for their trips, but we welcomed them all. We put them up and chatted long into the night with them. In short, I savoured some of the advantages of colonial life, even if in a most benighted place.

Our life soon settled down. We discovered a reservoir up in the hills and would often go there for a bathe in the afternoon. Some of the team went hunting pig and deer. Some local peasants were worried by wild boar raiding their crops and asked for help. I volunteered and began going out before dawn to a hide in a tree in the hope of shooting a boar. I saw some, but never hit any!

The district was fairly quiet. The peasants tended their crops and brought produce for sale into the village market and into the camps. The internee who had been the district administrator before 1941 visited his former subordinates. They welcomed him effusively, congratulated him on his survival and talked of how things would all get 'back to normal' before too long. I met the head man of Bangkinang and the 'captain' of the Chinese community. The Japanese had withdrawn into their camps and were not interfering much with the local people. There was not much to disturb the rural calm.

One incident did exercise me. The local police brought in two Japanese soldiers who had deserted with their rifles and a machine gun. I called Captain Hashimoto to my office and issued a stern reprimand. I – and Lord Louis Mountbatten – expected him, I said, to see that such disgraceful incidents did not recur. I handed the soldiers over to him for punishment and confiscated the machine gun. He apologised profusely and left with the two delinquents. The following day Dr Kukubu came to see me and presented me with a small cake with pink icing. I did not know what to make of this, so I accepted it gravely and put it aside fearing it might be poisoned. Then Dr Vaandrager explained that this was standard Japanese etiquette and demonstrated that the incident was officially closed. So I said no more, and tried the cake; it was revoltingly sweet.

Although everything in Bangkinang was within walking distance, it soon became clear that motor transport was going to be important for us. There were vehicles around, but all old and unsatisfactory. We were told that there had been no new vehicles in Sumatra since the Japanese conquest in 1941. At that time the Japanese army had brought with them little more than their guns. Anything else which they needed, they took; cars, trucks, bicycles, houses. They set up printing presses and printed money ('Japanese guilders') and paid for everything with these. When they arrived they had taken over a number of American cars and Dutch trucks, but after three years of incompetent driving many of these had broken down and there were no spares. However, there were skilled mechanics in the internment camps and at Bangkinang there was a workshop run by an able Dutchman named Reints. It was his boast that he could put any vehicle back on the road, even if only for an hour. He was a very skilled mechanic and had assembled an excellent team. They could remake almost any broken part of any engine.

Shortly after our arrival, Langley demanded money and transport from the Japanese headquarters, and these soon arrived; a massive Buick eight-cylinder limousine, two trucks and several thousand newly printed guilders. With these we managed through the months that followed.

We were just settled into Bangkinang and were getting our things in order when an astonishing message came through. Lady Mountbatten was going to visit our camp! We were all amazed and most were delighted, though I was dismayed at the thought of a grand visitation – I had memories of inspections by royalty and by visiting generals in England. I thought it would mean fuss and protocol, smart uniforms, standing in line in the sun while a grandee swept by making pointless remarks.

We had two days to prepare, and worked desperately. We tried to find out something about her. Who was she? Why was she coming? What were we supposed to do? Most of what we could find out was mere gossip. She was the wife of the glamorous Lord Louis Mountbatten, the famous captain of the destroyer *Kelly*, head of combined operations and now supreme allied commander South East Asia, and a member of the royal family, a cousin of the king. She had been a famous society beauty in earlier days with a scandalous reputation. She was a high-up officer in the Red Cross. She was indefatigable. She was visiting all the internment camps in the Far East to 'see for herself'.

We cleared up our quarters and prepared a room for her. We had a new lavatory built at the back (ours, with squat holes, was hardly suitable). We tried to put together a suitable meal. We tried to answer the anxious Dutch questions about precedent and protocol for receiving a member of the British royal family.

Then came the day, 16 September, and she arrived – a lean, gaunt woman in a stained uniform of the St John's Ambulance, bearing a general's insignia. She was accompanied by a large Sikh major as ADC. We were told that she had started out with a lady in waiting, but that the feeble creature had collapsed early on in the tour! Lady Louis immediately started enquiring how many people we had and what their conditions were. She rapidly dispensed with the elaborate reception and introductions that had been arranged and demanded to see the camps. She spent four hours going round both camps in full midday tropical sun and spoke to at least 200 people. Everywhere she enquired tenderly of how they were, how long they had been in the camps and how their health was. She insisted on climbing up into the barrack where Mevrow Holle lay sick with dysentery in order to consult with her. I accompanied her everywhere, and I was exhausted. I was amazed at her stamina, her grace and charm. Then she got into her jeep and swept off again to Pakanbaroe and her plane back to Singapore.

The effect on the camps was very powerful. Not only were they charmed and delighted by her grace, courtesy and manifest interest, but they were also tremendously uplifted. For three years they had seen and heard nothing. They feared that everyone had forgotten them and that no one cared what happened to them, and that they were doomed to rot forever in the steaming jungles. But now a member of the British royal family had come personally to Bangkinang – the end of the earth – to see them and to enquire of their welfare! They were not forgotten after all! Somebody important did care! Perhaps things might some day come right for them.

THE JAPANESE

A major part of my experiences in Sumatra was my relations with the Japanese. As I have said, when I went in I knew very little about these enemies of ours – though of course I had been filled for years with propaganda. In the thirties, I had heard tales of the ant-like workers who captured world markets by making shoddy goods, cheap bicycles and rubbishy clothing. Later came tales of fiendish yellow warriors who had spread southward through China conquering the cities and showing appalling brutality. Then the wartime tales. First their amazing victories when an army of yellow men swept aside Europeans with contemptuous ease, capturing Hong Kong, Indo China, Malaysia and Singapore and then going on to capture the Dutch East Indies and Burma. We were told that they had uncanny skill as jungle fighters and extraordinary oriental wiles. There were also the victories of their air force who had caught the Americans napping and annihilated their fleet at Pearl Harbor, who had sunk the two greatest battleships of the British Navy, the *Prince of Wales* and the *Repulse* in one afternoon. The Japanese seemed invincible. Then gradually had come other tales – of great cruelty – mass rapes of nurses in Hong Kong, barbarities to prisoners of war. There were many films, especially from America, showing them as malignant dwarfs, all wearing spectacles, with mouths full of glittering golden teeth, waving swords and being blown up by John Wayne. Gradually our armies and fleets had tackled theirs and defeated them in Burma, and in the Pacific War. It appeared that the Japanese could be defeated, but was it only because of our superior equipment? Apparently their soldiers never surrendered, fighting to the last, starving, committing suicide rather than surrendering (as Germans,

Italians, Russians, Frenchmen and Englishmen were all prepared to do when things were hopeless). What sort of people were they? Army information pamphlets ('Know your Enemy') about the Japanese were not as informative as earlier ones about the Germans had been. I had known many Germans before I fought them, but I had never known a Japanese. I wondered what on earth I would find.

Now suddenly I was face to face with the reality. Just up the road from our quarters was the camp of the former guards of the internment camp. I saw them exercising, lounging about, cooking their food. I soon had to have meetings with them, to get goods we needed. They were invariably polite and smiling, and apparently willing to help. I met Captain Hashimoto in charge, a mild grey haired bespectacled man, his medical officer, Dr Kukubu, the quartermaster, Lieutenant Hori and the former guards, a collection of untidy little men in brown uniforms, with peaked caps, puttees and big boots. Their discipline in the camp seemed poor; there was no proper guard on the gate. Most of them were pottering around, many stripped to the waist. They were a motley crew, mostly unshaven and many looking seedy and unfit. The NCOs seemed particularly nasty – solid brutal looking men with shaven heads, thick necks, coarse faces and large swords.

At the first meetings there was a great deal of bowing and smiling but very little communication. I spoke in English to Ledeboer, who spoke in Dutch to his interpreter, who spoke in Malay to Captain Hashimoto's interpreter who then passed the message on in Japanese. Except for insisting that even more fresh food be sent into the camps we could do little.

I began, however, to take notice of these Japanese and wonder about them. The first observations were the obvious ones. The Japanese were physically as different from one another as Europeans. Some were the stereotype bespectacled grinning dwarfs, but others were tall, some were fat, some dark brown, some pale yellow. Soon I got to know and recognise some of them. They were invariably polite, bowing and smiling whenever they saw me. Communication was difficult, though some of the officers spoke halting English. They seemed anxious to be correct. I could not tell how they felt, but there seemed to be no sullen

86

resentment, merely difficulty in understanding.

I began asking about the Japanese. All the internees resented and hated them, their conquerors and jailers. Many told stories of beatings and cruelties. Every Japanese soldier had demanded that internees bow before speaking and beat them if they failed to do it. But also there was puzzlement and attempts to understand and explain. Of the beatings, internees remarked that the Japanese did no more to them than they did to one another; Japanese sergeants regularly kicked and pummelled soldiers; senior officers slapped the faces and kicked the shins of junior officers. The internees also reported that often, the day after a beating, the Japanese soldier would give a small sweetmeat or cake to the person he had beaten. It appeared that this was to convey that there was nothing personal in the beating – it was merely necessary in the line of duty. Despite their severity to adults, the Japanese were very kind to the small children running about the women's camp, often giving them food and watching them play with fondness.

The prisoners of war from Pakanbaroe spoke of the Japanese in different tones from the internees. They told with bitter hatred of comrades who had been maliciously tortured, of desperately sick men sent out to work so that they collapsed and died, of horrible beatings and public executions. It was puzzling. Did Japanese soldiers perhaps feel that imprisoned civilians were somehow different from soldiers who had fought, had lost their battles and not committed suicide?

Still, we had to deal with them, and very difficult it was. We needed transport and they had it. We asked for it but nothing came. We raged and shouted and they kept apologising and smiling. I felt puzzled and angry. Then came relief. One day, at one of these interminable meetings in the Japanese camp, a new face appeared. A lanky Japanese, bearing the insignia of a sergeant, approached me and said in fluent English with a strong American accent, 'Pardon me, sir, but are you by any chance Captain Kerrack, sir?' Somewhat surprised, I said I was Captain Clark; he looked at his notebook and remarked, 'These stoopid ideograms; they can never write "L". Allow me to introduce myself – Myazawa Nobuo, sergeant interpreter. I have been sent down here from command headquarters at Bukit Tingi in the hope that I can help. I gather you have some kind of communication problem with the good Captain Hashimoto here.' And he smiled broadly at my tiresome counterpart.

Thus began a strange friendship which enriched my days in Sumatra. Nobuo Myazawa was an intelligent, educated gentleman slightly older than me. He was the son of a Japanese diplomat who had been stationed in Washington and he had been educated in the United States. When he finally returned to Japan in 1940 he had been regarded with grave suspicion by the Kempeitai, the dreaded thought police; they arranged his conscription into the army and posting overseas, as well as ensuring that he should not be an officer. He had a dreary and lonely time in the garrison of Sumatra. Then suddenly in June 1945 his fluent English became of value and he was in constant demand as an interpreter. He was often attached to me and we took some long journeys together. I think that he was delighted to have someone to whom he could talk freely after years of holding his tongue; I was delighted to have someone to answer my many questions. Two lonely characters marooned among comrades whom we regarded as philistines, we felt great sympathy for each other. He delighted in explaining Japanese ways and customs to me, often regarding them with western contempt. I recall after one particularly trying and frustrating conference he remarked as we got into my jeep, 'You know, Cap'n, these goddam Japanese, they make me sick!'

Myazawa and I talked about many things – the books we had read and enjoyed, the places we had seen, this strange and horrible war that had swallowed up our youth. He was interested to learn what English people knew of and thought of, Japan. He was fascinated to hear that we had a light opera entitled *The Mikado* (he giggled at this piece of lèse-majesté), but when I whistled the theme tune he was amazed, exclaiming, 'But that's the marching song of the men of Kyushu – all of us learn that in kindergarten'.

Most interesting to me, however, was what he told me about life in the Japanese army. He told me of his savage induction training, of the beatings and humiliations. 'My shins were black with bruises from the sergeants' kicks for the whole two months of basic training.' He said that the peasant conscripts with him were not bothered by this; they had had worse from their fathers. He told how the soldiers accepted that when they were drafted overseas their duty was to die for the emperor and the nation. They put their affairs in order and destroyed all mementoes. They did not carry photos of their families or sweethearts, as we did, lest it weaken their resolve. I had shown him mine; he had none to show me. He spoke of their great respect for anyone who died in battle; this brought automatic posthumous promotion and enshrinement in the great Yasukuni shrine in Tokyo.

He told me of the plans made for the last fight for Sumatra. They knew they would be defeated and that they would all die; that was their fate and their task. The challenge was to kill as many allied soldiers as possible in the process. As an English speaker he was told to strap dynamite sticks around his waist, to penetrate the enemy lines giving greetings in English, get as near as possible to a group of officers and then blow himself and them up. When I expressed amazement at this assignment he was surprised; it seemed to him a perfectly reasonable task to give to a front line soldier for the last desperate battle.

He told me of the consternation caused two months earlier by the news that Japan had surrendered. At first no one believed it; they felt sure it was an American propaganda trick and they determined to fight on and to the death, as was their manifest duty. Then a prince of the imperial house flew to Singapore with a copy of the imperial rescript and they had to admit that the unbelievable was true. They were even more confused by the imperial order which forbade suicide and stated that anyone who did kill themselves would be denied a place in the national soldiers shrine. This caused great moral conflict – on the one hand suicide was clearly the correct and ethical course, on the other, the emperor himself (and all his generals) had forbidden it. What should an honourable man do? Myazawa himself had had little difficulty in deciding to stay alive (after all, he was American raised and only a sergeant) but many of the officers agonised over the dilemma. The few who did take the honourable course and killed themselves were much admired for their integrity (though of course they were officially disgraced).

As I listened to all this, I was amazed and perplexed. Here were

89

young men like me of my age in an army quite like ours and yet so different.

POLITICS INTERVENE

At first, I thought that our task, my task, was simple; sort out the internees, get them into a good state and get them back to civilisation where they would make a good recovery.

That was what had been done for the British prisoners of war in Pakanbaroe. They were fed, clothed, assessed and flown off to India and back to England. It seemed easy. This process had gone ahead smoothly and the camps soon emptied. Major Boitteaux decided that his work was done, and on 4 October he departed, taking Ian Barclay with him. Langley, now a major, was appointed officer in charge of Pakanbaroe as well as Bangkinang and moved himself there.

At first it seemed we could do the same for the Dutch and Eurasian internees in the Bangkinang camps. We saw that they had adequate food and were delighted to see their skinny bodies filling out. We arranged air drops of clothing, medicines, essential supplies. We got mail in and out. We got them clothing and personal belongings. They seemed to be getting back to normal. We encouraged them to arrange parties and dances. It would soon be time to move them.

But where? They were East Indians. A few wanted to go back to Holland, but they were reminded that it was a devastated, hungry land. The Germans had bombed the towns in 1940, fought through the country and flooded the polders in 1944, starved the people in the winter of 1944–5. There was not much for anyone there. Most of the people in the camps wanted to go back to the good life they had known before 1941 when they were the privileged administrators of a vast, rich, fertile land, where they had lived well with plenty of Malay servants and worked as doctors, judges, policemen, plantation owners, administrators. But would that be possible?

In Malaysia the British army moved in and provided administrators for the liberated territories, but in Sumatra it was different. The British army did not come – to Bangkinang at any rate. An Indian brigade had landed at Padang, on the west coast, but showed little inclination to move inland. Hardly anyone came out from Holland. There was no sign of the royal Dutch army or navy. The internees began to mutter. What were the British doing? Why did they not let them take over once again? Were the British planning to take advantage of Holland's weakness to steal the Netherlands Indies and add them to their empire?

Then gradually, a new factor intervened. In early October we heard over the wireless that in Java an Indonesian republic had been set up. A number of Indonesian nationalists led by a Dr Soekarno, whom the Dutch had imprisoned before the war, had been released by the Japanese during the occupation and had now set up as a government; they had proclaimed a republic and said they would resist the Dutch return. The Japanese generals in Java had handed a lot of military equipment, guns, trucks and ammunition over to them.

This news came to Bangkinang slowly, but the leaders of the camp asked me about the intentions of Lord Louis Mountbatten, of SEAC, of the British government in England, none of whom had bothered to tell me what they were intending. I could only reply that my task was to look after the internees and get them safely out of the jungle, and that I was determined to do that. I had nothing to do with revolutions.

At first the Dutch thought it unlikely that the freedom ('merdeka') movement would spread to Sumatra, but it soon became clear that it would – there was talk of unrest in Padang and in Bukit Tingi. Soon came reports of discussions and agitation in the villages along the road, in Payakoemboe and Moeara Mahat, in Bangkinang and Pakanbaroe and the red and white flag of the Merdeka Party was flown in the village. In the vegetable market the vendors became sullen and we had to advise people from the camps not to go alone into the villages. Gradually the tension mounted. There were tales of attacks on Dutch people who had gone back to their former homes. We received orders from Padang to watch the situation with great care, and to avoid clashes between the ex-internees and the local Malay population.

Policy about evacuation of the Bangkinang camps changed several times. Groups of people who wanted to go to other parts of Sumatra, such as Palembang and Medan, or to Java, were moved to Pakanbaroe and evacuated by air. But most of our people belonged to central Sumatra. Gradually the idea of evacuating them by road over the mountains to Padang emerged.

But this was a difficult task. Though well engineered, the road was rough and long and difficult. At Rantaubrangin, 40 km from Bangkinang the road crossed the Siak River; there was a big wooden bridge built by the Japanese in 1942 but this was now so rickety and unsafe that the only way to get the trucks across the river was by a primitive ferry on a cable. After crossing the low-lands, the road climbed a range of steep mountains with many hairpin bends, at one point nine of them one above the other. After crossing the highland plateau to Bukit Tungi it went down the far side to Padang by the sea – a journey of about 250 km, taking up to 12 hours.

The only transport available was that of the Japanese army, a motley collection of worn out vehicles captured in 1941 and badly maintained since. British army HQ in Padang sent Miss Joan Bamforth Fletcher over to Bangkinang to manage the evacuation. She was a massive forthright Canadian, who was a member of the Field Ambulance and Nursing Yeomanry (FANY). She rapidly displayed great organising ability and an overpowering personality. What she wanted, she got. If there was any argument, she 'went to the top'. She was a personal friend of the brigadier in command of the British troops in Padang and never hesitated to involve him.

Langley told me to take charge of the convoy arrangements and this kept me busy for weeks. Before each convoy there were conferences, attended by the Japanese officers in charge of the convoy, the senior internees, Miss Fletcher, myself and many other interested people such as Captain Hashimoto, who insisted on a receipt for any internees removed. There were endless difficulties. The convoys had to start in the small hours, in order to get over the river before the water rose with the afternoon rain. The trucks had to go across by the ancient ferry, causing even more delays. Trucks broke down and had to be repaired.

Before the very first convoy there was a crisis. The Japanese drivers stayed put in their camp; we found out that they had heard that a woman was to be in charge of the convoy! They felt this was a deliberate insult and they refused to start. Not until I had explained that Miss Fletcher had the rank of an officer and a captain in the British army would they go. When they returned from Padang I asked nervously how it had gone, only to find that the Japanese now held her in high esteem. I was told that when the convoy arrived in Padang, the internees were welcomed by their relatives but the Indian soldiers were very hostile to the Japanese drivers and wanted to put them in gaol. Fletcher was furious and stormed through the garrison, right up to the brigadier insisting on proper accommodation and good food for 'her Japanese'. She got it, then and on later trips, and they were her devoted servants! My friend, Myazawa, was a great help to her.

I went to Padang with the third trip, a fascinating journey. It was the first time since landing that I had got out of the steaming jungle. We travelled on the flat for a while, then came to the bridge and the ferry. We all got out and hung around while the trucks were ferried across. After that the road began to climb and we crossed the equator. The point was marked by a Japanese memorial, a concrete globe, set up to commemorate the moment in 1941 when their conquering armies had entered the southern hemisphere. We crossed the first ridge of mountains and wound down the other side, negotiating all the dreadful hairpins. In the highlands came blessed relief for me as the weather grew cooler and atmosphere less oppressive; suddenly my prickly heat stopped prickling and I felt well for the first time in weeks. In the central plateau around Bukit Tingi the country was quite different – well cultivated fields, prosperous looking villages, cattle, goats and lively looking people. Bukit Tingi was a pleasant town, with wide streets, many shady trees and handsome bungalows and colonial residences. It had been the favourite hill town for the administrators and merchants of Padang and the administrative headquarters for Central Sumatra.

Then down the western slopes and a final run through the verdant paddy fields of the coastal plain, until we came into Padang, port, city and beach head of the British forces, a brigade of the 26th Indian Division. Allied soldiers everywhere, smartness, saluting, military police, traffic direction signs. I stayed overnight in the officers' mess of the field ambulance, a friendly group of British and Indian doctors relaxing after years of bitter fighting in the Burma jungles. I made the trip many times, first with the ex-internees and then with other groups.

It was on one of the later trips that one of my strangest experiences with the Japanese occurred. By now, the Japanese seemed to be at ease with me. They offered me some of their lunch – of boiled sticky white rice, dried fish and vegetables – and were amazed when I handled the chopsticks with ease. The returning convoy was late in starting and was slowed by many breakdowns. By evening we were still in the highlands. There was a long discussion amongst the Japanese officers and then Myazawa came to me and said, 'We cannot go further tonight. The camp of these soldiers is near here. Captain Takayama asks would you care to spend the night in their camp?' I thought, why not? and accepted. We drove a few miles to the camp – wooden buildings in a clearing – and I was shown into a clean room with a pleasant view. Would I like a bath? Yes, I said. A cold bath or a hot bath? I said I would prefer a cold bath, and the officers and I all went down to the bath house, where we stripped off, soaped ourselves and then splashed around in a delightful cool pool. Then, dressed in fresh clothes, we had dinner. The colonel, now wearing a kimono, cooked the meal himself – a delightful dish of meat and fish and vegetables cooked in broth in front of us (later I learned that this was called Sukiyaki). I ate it with genuine delight, praising it the while and relishing the rice wine with which they plied me. After dinner they sang sad songs accompanied by a sort of mandolin and showed me the copy books in which they were practising their calligraphy. After a delightfully peaceful night's sleep (free of sweating and prickly heat) we ran down peacefully to Bangkinang to prepare for the next convoy.

It was not until some weeks later, when he knew me better, that Myazawa revealed some of the anxieties that had lain behind that pleasant evening. The Japanese officers had used up the last of their precious stock of Japanese sake to toast me. The ingredients of the Sukiyaki had also been very difficult to obtain, and they were amazed at the amount I had eaten. In one point, however, I had done well: 'You gained great face about the bath', he said. 'What do you mean?' 'Well, of course, everyone knew you would rather have a hot bath. But they were impressed by your sensitivity and delicacy; they saw that you realised that it would take hours to prepare a hot bath and so you most considerately said you preferred a cold bath.' I was amazed. I had opted for a cold bath because that was what I wanted! But I had been credited with a tact and delicacy which I never had! How many other gaffes might I have committed! What a complex world the orient was!

Meanwhile, the Indonesian revolution was spreading. There had been trouble in Padang and Bukit Tingi – would it come to Bangkinang?

One day, a Dutch officer from the camp came over to me in great alarm. His men had been tapping the local telephone line (which ran past the camp). On it they had overheard politicians from Bukit Tingi giving instructions to the local Bangkinang branch of the Merdeka Party to proclaim the revolution, run up the red and white flag and seize the town – tomorrow. What was I going to do? Did I realise that the only weapons in the district (ten carbines) were in the Bangkinang police station?

Hurried conferences occurred. Here was an urgent crisis and they looked to me as the British officer to solve it. I realised that if I did not act there would probably be an attack on the camp and that some of the people I was responsible for might be harmed – or killed. I put on my best and smartest uniform, I got out my automatic, collected a competent Dutch interpreter and a group of husky ex-soldiers and set off for the village. There I called a conference at the police station, the village headman, an elderly white haired Malay, the captain of the local Chinese merchants, the leader of the local Freedom Party, the local mullah and the village police sergeant, an anxious little man in uniform.

There was at first some confused parleying, but then I delivered myself of a speech. I said that I was acting on the Direct Authority of the Supreme Commander of South East Asia; that it was my

96

Duty to see that Law and Order were maintained; that I had heard that Unruly Elements were considering Disturbing the Peace, and that therefore in order to Preserve Law and Order I was impounding the police armoury. To my astonishment no one demurred; the police sergeant merely asked if he could have a receipt. We removed the ten carbines and their ammunition and a bundle of sabres and withdrew to the camp.

The ex-soldiers with me, dark swarthy villains, who I was told were Ambonese, were delighted to have weapons again and became my devoted bodyguard. They moved into the compound of our bungalow and constituted themselves a guard company. They drilled happily, mounted a sentry at the gate and turned out the guard every time I walked through the gate.

During these weeks the news of the revolution became steadily more alarming. We heard that the Freedom Party had occupied much of Java, including Jakarta (formerly Batavia) the capital, and that they had attacked British troops who were holding Javanese ports. Then we heard of increasing trouble in Padang. Dutch ex-internees were being attacked; a family from the Bangkinang camp had been found floating in a Padang canal with their throats cut. Tension was rising among the British troops. The brigadier set up a perimeter, withdrew his troops into barracks, established a curfew and forbade his officers to go out 'swanning' (unauthorised trips). But he got little cooperation from the local townspeople who seemed unwilling to hand over evildoers or to co-operate in maintaining the peace.

Then came several frightening incidents. Some members of a RAPWI team in northern Sumatra, who had been out in the country, were killed, including the medical officer. It was said that they were looking for emeralds; but they had certainly been speared. Then came the worst incident. The brigade in Padang had welcomed the welfare ladies and women members of the RAPWI organisation as lending interest and charm to their many parties. One of the liveliest was a St John's Ambulance officer, who became very friendly with the brigade major. One day they took a jeep and set off for a swim and a picnic beyond the perimeter. They did not return. The jeep was traced to a seaside village – but there was no further sign of them. No one knew anything.

As I heard the story later, the brigadier blew up at this point. The brigade major had been a personal friend through many months of war. As an English gentleman, the brigadier felt very protective toward the welfare ladies. He sent some of his toughest troops down to the village. They lined up the men of the village and interrogated them in order; when the headman remained silent they shot him. They then shot the next three until one broke down and showed them the corpses of the brigade major and the welfare lady, heavily mutilated, buried in a nearby ravine. Further questioning established that they had been chopped to death by an excited mob of villagers. They shot the men who had revealed the bodies and threw them in the grave, and burned the village.

The British officers were divided – most approving, some fearful, some disgusted. To their surprise, the civilians in Padang were delighted. The mayor and the captain of the Chinese community called on the brigadier to congratulate him and promise full co-operation. Until then, they said, they did not know whether the British meant what they said. Now they could see that they did and they could see that they were going to stay. That evening the chief of police of Padang delivered to the jail most of the leaders of the freedom movement who he had been 'quite unable to find' for the previous two months.

When I heard these tales I began to wonder what I might have to do in Bangkinang, and felt very glad that I had impounded the guns! The village of Bangkinang remained quiet, though sullen.

We realised that life in Sumatra was getting steadily more dangerous for British soldiers. We noticed that the villagers who used to look at us benignly or wave cheerfully were now often scowling. But we were comfortable in our vehicles, well armed and fairly secure. Personally I felt bold and prepared to take chances; I had survived so many greater hazards during the last year. On one occasion, however, danger brushed near.

Atherton and I were driving back to Bangkinang from Padang on 20 October. We were in the big Buick which was running well. We made good time up to Bukit Tingi where we spent a blessed cool night in the hotel. Next morning we set off on the trip back. We got over the mountains and were running briskly through some paddy fields outside the village of Moeara Mahat when a water buffalo suddenly lurched across the road; Atherton put on the brakes and they failed. The big car smashed into the buffalo which scampered off bellowing. We examined the front of the car which was sadly dented, but the engine was still running, so we drove on. Soon steam was pouring from the bonnet; we stopped again and discovered that the fan had cut into the radiator which was spouting fountains of water all over the engine. So there we were, with a broken car, in a hostile countryside. A crowd began to gather, at first merely curious, but then gradually turning unfriendly. A spokesman – presumably the village school teacher – pushed forward and began to try to talk to us. First he tried Malay, but we had none. Then he tried Dutch; I was about to respond but suddenly realised that this might identify us as colonial oppressors. So I went back to Malay pidgin and gesticulation, insisting that we were not *'Orang Belanda'* (Dutchmen) but *'Orang Ingrish'* (Englishmen) and asked him to telephone for help to Pakanbaroe. We were still making little progress when a truck full of Japanese soldiers came up the road and stopped to see what was happening. The sergeant saluted me briskly and looked helpfully at the leaking radiator, but communication here was even more limited. However, he summoned the driver of his truck – a squat cheerful figure with an extremely ugly and nearly black face – and indicated that he should deal with the problem. I had an interesting consultation with this mechanic. We had only two phrases in common – 'OK' the universal phrase of approval, and *'tidda bagush'*, the Malay phrase for 'it doesn't go'. With these two we managed perfectly. I pointed to the parts – he gave them names in Japanese American – I said whether they were 'OK' or *'tidda bagush'*. He heaved the fan off the radiator and knocked its blades back in alignment with a heavy hammer. He then looked at the leaks in the radiator and blocked them with a paste made of cotton waste, engine oil and cold boiled rice from his lunch tin. We filled the radiator with water from the ditch, stopped a few more leaks and drove off cautiously back to Bangkinang, escorted by our cheerful Japanese friends.

During October the weather was getting steadily worse. The rains, at first spasmodic, now came regularly every day in the middle of the afternoon. The morning was hot and dusty as ever, with blinding sunlight. In the early afternoon a great black cloud could be seen coming up from the south west advancing from the mountains. Along its front, lightning flickered and thunder rumbled. Just before it reached us there would be a storm of violent wind, scattering leaves, blowing away papers, tearing limbs off trees. Then came the thunder and lightning, banging all around, crash after crash. Then finally the rain, pouring down in a solid mass so that the roads were inches deep and the spray flew up head high. One could only cower under cover. After an hour or two it slackened and stopped and we all came out into the damp rather cooler evening to do our business.

The storms gave me a fright one evening in late October. Just as the thunder started we were sitting on our verandah. Suddenly there was a blinding flash and a simultaneous deafening crash of thunder. We had been hit by lightning! As we gathered ourselves, shaken, we smelled burning. In my bedroom the bed was on fire; as we dowsed it we saw that my wireless was blasted, blackened and fused onto the bedstead. The lightning had come down the aerial, through the wireless and onto the bed. Had I been listening to my radio, as I often did, I would have been dead.

SUMATRA REFLECTIONS

My feelings about myself, the army and what I was doing swung a great deal in Sumatra. At first I was excited and challenged. I was engaged on a great errand of mercy, rescuing and succouring the suffering. On 2 September, before setting off, I wrote to Mary Rose:

> It is a grand job, far better than I had hoped for. Parachuting into the prisoner-of-war camps in Japanese territory to help our lads there who are ill. The war is over, the Japs are being friendly and there is no danger. What a chance it will be to do some real medical work, to help someone who really needs help instead of mucking about doing parades and suchlike nonsenses . . .

I was going to do medical work; I was serving with a *corps d'elite*, the seasoned partisan warriors: I was seeing the exotic east at first hand, far away from the dull confines of army cantonments. It was exotic, new and exciting.

I spent a lot of time talking to the internees, both individually and in groups. The doctors invited me to tell them about the new wonder drugs, especially penicillin, which had been discovered and developed after they went into internment. I was invited to talk to camp audiences about what had happened in Holland during the war; the last news they had had was of the fall of their Motherland in 1940. I was able to tell them of the battle of Arnhem, the battles of the Rhine delta, the flooding of the polders, of my own service in Limbourg in January 1945, and of the final liberation. I also talked long to many fascinating individuals about the Netherlands Indies, their long history (of which I had known nothing), their enlightened colour policy (compared with British India) and the great colonial traditions especially in Java and Batavia.

But then the excitement began to ebb. Nothing seemed to be happening. Langley bustled about, full of mystery, while I just sat in Bangkinang. No letters came, though I wrote regularly to my mother and to Mary Rose. There was no medical work for me to do. My prickly heat pricked all day. On 25 October I became ill with a high fever and a rash and awful pains in my limbs. Dr Vaandrager came to see me and diagnosed 'five day fever'. He said there was no treatment but aspirins and that it would go away. It did but it was very unpleasant while it lasted. I became despondent and depressed.

On one occasion Atherton and I gave a party for our friends in the camp and had made a punch based on Chinese gin and local fruit juices. The younger internees, especially the pretty girls, were dancing to an old gramophone and the older people were singing 'Vaterlands liedjes' – the old songs like 'Piet Hein'. Suddenly I was overwhelmed with acute misery and went to my bunk and sobbed. I knew I would die in these horrible jungles and never see my home again; if I did get back Mary Rose would have married another; all the jobs in medicine would have gone; nothing would ever come right for me again. I can still recall the black horror of that evening as the firelight flickered through the lattice work on my window. This melancholia had passed by the following morning, but recurred after the next party and I realised that I was having some sort of toxic reaction – perhaps an interaction between the locally made 'gin' (said to contain methyl alcohol) and the mepacrine I took every morning (against malaria).But it was a frightening pit of gloom to fall into.

Even after the acute misery passed I still felt sad and useless. Langley assured me that I was doing an excellent job but I could not believe him, so he sent me on a convoy to Padang. When I came back I found the Bangkinang camp in turmoil. The Dutch doctors were furious with Atherton who, they said, had overridden and insulted them. Ledeboer had left in a fury because he had been overruled. I realised that by just being there , an officer, a doctor, an Englishman, in touch with headquarters, I was performing a useful function. I decided to stay and finish the job and get all 'my people' away to safety in Padang . Langley told me how much he needed me to hold together the Bangkinang end of his command. He told me to look my part; to put up my campaign ribbons and to put my parachute wings on my chest, like a proper irregular warrior. With these additions I now looked very different, dressed in green combat jacket and trousers, wearing a broad brimmed Australian hat and padding along in tattered boots patched with native rubber. I wore a low slung belt with a Browning automatic on my left hip and a long American 'killing knife' on the right. When I went on trips I carried a carbine and a cutlass, a truly piratical figure.

I took firm control of Bangkinang, dealing with the Japanese, keeping the village quiet and getting the convoys away twice a week. I became more involved in the problems of vehicle maintenance, learning surprising skills, such as how to stop a truck that had no brakes (double declutch down through the gears until it stalls) and how to start a limousine with no starter and no cranking handle (get a group of villagers to push it).

My feelings about myself and my work went up and down. Two extracts from my diary show my varying moods. On 23 October I wrote:

I have now been here 6 weeks and apart from a lack of mail it has been a most pleasant time. Materially I live well, spiritually I am monarch of all I survey and I like that. Financially it hasn't cost me a penny. I reckon I must have accumulated about £150 in three months since I left England. Experiences – Lady Louis, Hashimoto, Boitteaux, Myazawa, Mohammed Mazouki and little Hori. I reckon I have done a good job of work too. I prefer this to doctoring – not nearly so difficult. What a change – what a glorious change from 6 Airborne Div. 5 Para Brigade sit in Singapore doing masses of police duties . . . I am very well out of that. I shall try my very damnedest to stay with this RAPWI as long as possible.

On 27 October during 5 day fever I was in more sombre mood:

I realise how many political ideals and morals I myself have lost – so young. I have no hope at all of 'peace'. I am certain that there will be another war that will kill as this one has done; I am quite accustomed to concentration camps, torture, secret police etc. as normal means of government. I have accepted the dread formula that the end justifies the means and am quite prepared to excuse and even use Nazi methods of politics. I regard force as being the only final arbiter of anything and Justice, Freedom and Liberty as relative symbols in the class struggle, without any intrinsic value of their own. I am sure I am right in all these views, as a convinced materialist and a rather untutored dialectical one. But what a barren prospect! What a fine life for MRH and me and our children! And nothing to do about it.

I found a pleasant epitaph in the book by Piet van Paassens:

> *Ik leef en weet niet hoe lang,*
> *Ik sterf en weet niet wanneer,*
> *Ik reis en weet niet waarheen,*
> *Vreemd dat ik zoo vroolijk ben!*

> I live and know not how long
> I die and know not why,
> I travel and know not whither,
> Strange that I am so cheerful!

Langley had become very actively involved in plans and intrigues. He was constantly in conclaves with former Dutch administrators and soldiers and off on trips to Singapore and Padang. From one of these he brought me a fine camera and a handful of $50 American gold pieces – 'A little something that has come my way'. He told me he valued my support and comradeship; he was putting together a 'stay-behind' team to work to frustrate the revolutionaries; would I join him? I was quite tempted. It was nice to be valued and to be asked to help. It was romantic and secret. But I wanted to get home and get back to doctoring and so I gracefully declined.

Then came another project. All over Sumatra were groups of Javanese coolies, starving, diseased and dying. They were originally brought over by the Japanese. Now, no one wanted them. The Sumatran revolutionaries were happy to see them die. I visited some in a camp near Pakanbaroe. A few devoted Dutchmen were trying to help them. I had never seen such suffering – stick-thin limbs bloated with beriberi; scrotums swollen to the size of footballs with oedema; ulcers that had eroded legs so far that the feet were gangrened. They just sat in passive apathy, waiting to die. Langley asked me to join him and a team to move round Sumatra forcing the Japanese to care for these unfortunates and ship them back to Java. I agreed to join, but then nothing came of it.

Politically I was dismayed and uncertain. In England in 1944 issues had seemed simple. Mary Rose and I were committed socialists. We were committed to the defeat of Nazi fascism, and to the overthrow of Japanese imperialism. We were working for a post war socialist Britain, of fair shares, equality and welfare for all. We were against all imperialism and colonisation and hoped to see all empires disappear.

But in Sumatra in 1945 it was not so easy. The Indonesian revolution did not seem to be about caring for poor people (like the Javanese coolies). It was about killing Dutchmen and pursuing tribal feuds – Atjinese against Menangkebau, Ambonese against Javanese. The Dutch people whom I liked and admired for their courage and intelligence were devoted to restoring the Netherlands Empire; Langley was keen to help them and to involve me. What was I up to?

I had certainly learned that revolutions were not a time of excitement and advance but a confused miserable time of random killing, destruction and uncertainty in which the vulnerable – the old, the sick, the children – were the ones that suffered most.

PAKANBAROE

Gradually we got the people away from the Bangkinang camps to Padang. The camps were almost empty. My job there was nearly done. Then the last convoy left and I gave Captain Hashimoto his last receipt 'for persons'. The Bangkinang camps, recently so appallingly full of people, stood empty and silent. It was time for us to go. Langley told me to pack our goods and move up to Pakanbaroe; on 11 November Atherton and I moved into his headquarters, the 'Mountbatten Hotel'. This ramshackle building, the only hotel in Pakanbaroe, was run by enterprising Chinese. Three months earlier it had been the 'Victory Hotel' and the Japanese officers club.

We were a mixed bag of RAPWI remnants – Langley, Eetje Klinkhamer, Atherton, myself, several Dutch civilians, some wireless operators and a few RAF staff who were responsible for the airfield on which now stood one aged Dakota – our only link with Singapore and safety. I lived for a month in Pakanbaroe, acting as Langley's deputy, holding our little group together as things grew more dangerous and working on the regular convoys to Padang, arranging their despatch, checking the vehicles and especially the loads. There were several groups of people in Pakanbaroe who did not want to be left to the mercies of the Indonesians, such as British Indian shopkeepers and Chinese 'comfort girls'.

Life was becoming steadily more dangerous. A few days before there had been a dramatic incident which those who had seen it told me with wonder and delight. A crowd had assembled in downtown Pakanbaroe, and whipped up by agitators, had become a mob and had suddenly surged up the street to our hotel,

106

shouting and demanding that the hated Dutch flag be removed from the line of allied flags that hung along the front of the hotel. No one was in the hotel except some Dutchmen, who hid in the lavatory, three women and a couple of RAF wireless operators. Hundreds of excited Indonesians were milling about shouting slogans, waving sticks and even guns and looking steadily more menacing. An RAF corporal was nervously trying to parley when Langley drove up in his jeep. Pushing his way in through the mob and up the stairs he demanded to know what was going on. The leading agitator, who had a machine gun in his hands, pointed it at Langley. With a roar and a shout 'Don't point that gun at me, you silly little man!' Langley picked him up bodily and threw him over the banisters onto the crowd below. This had an electric effect. The agitator bolted, so did his comrades, and the whole mob followed them down the street. Peace fell on the 'Mountbatten Hotel' again and the Dutchmen emerged from the lavatory. Everyone was greatly relieved though Langley was not perturbed; 'It seemed the obvious thing to do', he said that night at dinner.

The following day there was a formal conference, which I attended, with the commander of the Japanese troops in the area. At this conference Langley expressed grave dissatisfaction at the failure of law and order; the Japanese commander apologised profusely and promised nothing like this would happen again. From then on we had a platoon of Japanese soldiers guarding the hotel, and a fixed machine gun pointing down the main street of Pakanbaroe. I carried a loaded automatic at all times and slept with it by my bed.

We continued to watch the situation. Just down the road at the Merdeka headquarters we could see the young men drilling with pikes. On one occasion when we heard that more riots might be blowing up, Flight-Lieutenant Terry took off in our Dakota and flew it down the main street of Pakanbaroe at roof height, while one of his crew threw empty beer bottles into the street. The crack of exploding bottles, the thunder of the engines and the vast size of the plane (at 50 feet) had a most salutary and quietening effect on the town.

However, we knew that our stay was getting increasingly perilous, as well as being pointless. Langley decided that the time had come to go. Everything was to be denied to the revolutionaries. The engines were taken off of the Dakota and put on a barge, which Terry took down the river and across to Singapore. We took the wheels off the derelict plane and sold them to Chinese merchant (to help to pay our hotel bill). There was still a sum outstanding, so I signed a promissory note on the British government (which finally caught up with me two years later in Scotland). We then set fire to the plane. We destroyed some of our transport and loaded all our goods and some of our friends on the last four trucks and set off, on 11 December, for the last time on the trip over the mountains to Padang.

SINGAPORE AND JAVA

Now at last I was back with the British army, after three full months 'beyond the perimeter'. I lodged once again with the 48th (Indian) Field Ambulance and settled back into army medical life. They were a friendly lot; Colonel Petter had known me at the RAMC Depot in 1943; one of the doctors, Dick Jones, was a fellow Edinburgh graduate. I started doing medical duties and attending their many excellent parties.

One great delight in Padang was a vast bundle of mail for me – three months' accumulation. I retreated to my room to read them and weep with homesickness. All was well; mother was still well and planning to move to Somerset. Ralph was in the Marines and due to be posted overseas; Gwen had qualified as a doctor and was doing her house jobs; June had started medicine. Mary Rose's love poured from every page of her letters – along with her increasing bewilderment at hearing nothing from me. They had grown so anxious about me that my mother had approached our Edinburgh MP, Sir Will Y. Darling, the haberdasher turned bookseller turned politician, to demand news of me. He told them that the war office had said in October that they had made enquiries and that I was fit and well. (Later it turned out that the enquiry had reached 225, who had no idea where I was and so just sent an anodyne reply!) I borrowed a typewriter and started writing back.

However, this was only temporary. I had to get back to my comrades and my unit. I had heard that they were in Singapore, so I agitated to be sent there. My posting came through and I flew out on 19 December. On the flight out I made this note in my diary as we flew over the jungles of Northern Sumatra:

They looked just the same as they did when we flew in months ago. How much has happened since then. What has happened to me personally is well worth thinking on. Three months in the tropics. Seeing the birth of revolution. Meeting my enemies intimately and realising how propaganda and lies had distorted them. Running a complete show of my own – what an amazing time!

Once in Singapore I hurried to SEAC headquarters and to the medical section. To my astonishment (and delight) I found that they did indeed know who and where I was. Behind the DADMS was a large board with the names of all the doctors in his command and there was a tag with my name on it! A great surprise. I had come to feel that everyone had forgotten me!

They told me that 5 Parachute Brigade, with my unit 225 Parachute Field Ambulance, was now in Batavia, in Java and that I should rejoin them. However, in the meantime I could join the 'residue' of 5 Parachute brigade here in Singapore.

I joined them and found a sad collection of sick misfits. When the Brigade went into Java they left in Singapore all men unfit for duty. Some had recovered and were keen to get back to their units. Others were clearly unfit for further tropical service. Others were awaiting court martials for various crimes committed in Singapore. All were demoralised, as were the group of officers in charge. I was at once involved in medical parades and medical boards. Most of the illnesses were skin diseases, especially infections exacerbated by the dripping heat. The main treatment was gentian violet and I seemed to spend all my days painting armpits and groins with the vivid purple dye.

It was here that I spend Christmas 1945, one of the dreariest of my life. We were in great tropical heat (about 90°F) and maximum (90%) humidity but we were given the full English Christmas dinner (specially flown out from England) – turkey, potatoes, peas, beer, plum pudding, whisky, the works. According to army tradition the officers served the men their Christmas dinners and I can still remember the naked backs, running with sweat and adorned with gentian violet graffiti over which I had to reach to lay the inappropriate food before them. In the afternoon all the officers got drunk; I joined them, in misery and self-disgust.

In due course our orders came for sailing to Java. The 'fit' members of the residues embarked on a troopship on 29 December leaving behind those happy men who had been deemed by medical boards to be 'unfit for further tropical duty'. After a brief journey of a few days we arrived off Batavia, Java. The brigade was on the move, however and on 9 January we went to Semarang, another flat eastern town, rather battered by shellfire.

It felt wonderful to be back in 225 amongst people who knew me – I felt that I had come home! They welcomed me; they had been hearing odd rumours about me for months and wondered what on earth I was up to; all the other RAPWI doctors had returned to their units months ago. I was reunited with my 'base luggage' – belongings that I had left in England half a year ago, thick winter uniforms, heavy boots and other useless things. However, I did get back my typewriter – the typewriter with the special 'SS' keys that I had 'acquired' in Germany. I started trying to operate it and to type out reports on my work in Sumatra.

The Unit had changed. There was a new colonel, J.C. Watts, a cheerful surgeon and RAMC regular. Gordon Kennedy was a major and second in command, and Ray Kirkham, my old comrade, was a section officer. The other officers were mostly new and I found myself the 'senior captain'. I settled in and began to take an interest in the problems of Semarang. I was put in charge of the officers' mess catering and had to go daily into the local bazaar to bargain with Malays and Chinese for fresh food for the officers' mess. Since the only money we had were devalued 'Japanese guilders' it was a long slow process.

Although I only spent four weeks with 225 in Java, it was an important time for reassessing my relationship with the army. When I was last with them, in May 1945, I had been one of the junior section officers in a well-knit, battle-experienced field ambulance. But then I had had five months away on a variety of tasks, including several months running my own show, being responsible for the welfare of 2,000 people. I was now the senior captain in a quite different unit, many of whom had not seen battle. Gordon Kennedy told me that if I managed things right I might soon be a major. He told me that my section had always been the best in the unit and that I would have been promoted earlier if I had not been so bumptious and garrulous. I realised that I must soon decide how much of myself to give to the army.

Before I could settle, however, a signal came from 6th Airborne Division headquarters, now in Palestine, demanding that I be sent back to the division forthwith. 225 had enough doctors, the division was short of experienced medical officers. So I started on my travels once again.

CROSSING HALF THE WORLD

I travelled from Semarang in Java to Sarafand in Palestine between 28 January and 22 February 1946. It was a strange journey.

I was given a 'movement order' – a slip of paper saying 'Capt. D.H. Clark RAMC is to proceed from Semarang Java to 6th Airborne Division Headquarters Sarafand Palestine' and I was told to make my way there. By that time there were British military transport systems spanning Europe, Africa and Asia and there were 'transit camps' at all major stopping points. With a movement order you went from one transit camp to another. At each point you had to see the transport office and find out whether they could move you toward your destination. Sometimes it was easy and quick, sometimes appallingly slow. If you were in a hurry and wanted to get to your destination it was infuriating. If you had no desire to arrive, it was a strange but not unpleasant limbo in which to spend a few days, weeks or months of your life. Tales were told of officers who spent many months in transit camps, enjoying the local life, and failing to return to units which did not want them. The transit camps varied; all provided a bed and meals, some were delightful, with club and swimming facilities, while others were set in sandy wastes at the edges of military airstrips.

By this time I was fairly cynical about the army and its dealings with me. I would have preferred to stay with 225 in Java; I knew of no good reason why anyone should want me in Palestine. But I had to go. I heard that Palestine was dangerous – but so was Java. My overriding aim was to survive till my demobilisation came up, sometime later in the year. I decided to go, passively, wherever

113

they sent me and try to see as much of the world as I could while I travelled.

The first trip, from Semarang to Singapore by aeroplane, was brief and easy. The transit camp in Singapore was a pleasant place, set in a grove by the sea. Singapore was as hot and sweaty as ever, maximum temperature, maximum humidity; I remember going for a swim and finding myself sweating in the water as I swam. Singapore was a strange muddle in those days. It was the headquarters of South East Asia Command, of Mountbatten and all his generals, but was essentially the colonial city described by Somerset Maugham but soiled by three years of Japanese occupation. There were few buildings above two stories, no air conditioning and everything was shabby. The famous Raffles Hotel was a NAAFI officers club, tatty and dilapidated, with British and Indian officers sipping John Collins and skinny seedy looking ex-internees in white shirts and shorts. On the streets were the soldiers of the 14th Army – Indians of many shapes, sizes and colours – and their British officers strutting around with swagger sticks. There were gangs of former Japanese soldiers being used as coolies, bullied and cursed at by grinning English guards. The Japanese peasant soldiers, as ever, were working hard and obediently and did not seem much worried by the abuse. There were a few Malays but everywhere were the Chinese, bustling, selling, buying and doing business, coolies sweating loads and pulling rickshaws, fat merchants operating shops, lean lively young men prattling good English and keen to do business, beautiful slinky girls with black hair, almond eyes, and cheongsams slit to the thigh.

Each morning I went to the transport office and enquired about my journey and each morning there was nothing. I was informed that many people were travelling westward to India and back to England and many of them had higher priorities than me. I began to despair of ever leaving the east. So I took thought; I retyped my movement order so that it said that Captain Clark was urgently required in Palestine and I submitted that. Within two days I was on a Dakota flying toward India. We flew up the Arakan coast to Burma where we spent the night in a jungle transit camp. Next day on to Calcutta and then to Delhi. By this time I had reflected on this journey and realised that there was no point in hurrying. I took a day off and explored the grandiose imperial avenues of New Delhi. Then down to Bombay. I had found out that my dear friend Gustav Born who had come to India as an army pathologist was at a transit camp at Nasik. I went up to visit him and persuaded him to come to Bombay for a few days leave with me. We stayed at the Taj Mahal Hotel and enjoyed ourselves together for a week. We had a joint photograph taken and sent it home to our delighted families.

Gus went back to Nasik and I began to explore the challenge of getting to Palestine. All the westward planes were filled with priority passengers. All boats to Egypt were full. The RTO sergeant, a tall cheerful Eurasian, took pity on me. 'Would you like to see Baghdad, sir?' he said and when I eagerly agreed, he fixed me up with surface travel all the way to Palestine. Train to Karachi, boat up the Persian Gulf to Shaiba, river boat to Baghdad, Nairn transdesert bus to Damascus and train to Tel Aviv. I set off on an intriguing journey, travelling through the decayed remnants of pre-war elegance and adventure, the world of T.E. Lawrence, Gertrude Bell and Agatha Christie. In Karachi, a dusty, dirty port town, I met some Indian parachutists and among them Ian Stokoe who had been at school and medical school with me. The boat journey, along the coast of Persia and up the smooth muggy Persian Gulf, was uneventful and I did not stay long in Shaiba, the dusty, hot, dreary port at the mouth of the Euphrates, known throughout the army as the ultimate punishment station, the 'arsehole of the world'. Baghdad, however, was fascinating; I visited the ruins of Nineveh and saw the excavations; I explored the souks; I even bought a Persian rug and sent it home. The Nairn bus was like any other bus, but the place we stopped at in the middle of the desert was a true oasis, with date palms, camels, hawk nosed Bedouin – just as in every film and romance.

Damascus was delightful – green and beautiful. A guide attached himself to me, hailing me constantly as 'My captain!' and took me all around – the street called Straight, the house where Paul rested, the souks, the bazaars. It was magical and dreamlike. He was an educated Syrian, fluent in Arabic, French and English. He told me how the Damascans loved the English

115

but feared the return of the French. 'Do not leave us, oh my captain!', he wailed piteously. Then I went by a funny little train through Galilee (where the hills were all green) down to the coast among orange groves laden with big yellow fruit to Haifa and then on to Sarafand.

I rushed to the 6th Airborne Division headquarters to the office of the medical services and announced my arrival. I was delighted to see an officer I knew, but dismayed when he said, 'David, what on earth are you doing here? You are supposed to be in Java with 225! You'd better get back there as soon as you can!' At first I thought it was a joke but then I realised he was serious. No one at divisional headquarters knew why I had been sent for, and they did not particularly want me! I had spent a month travelling across southern Asia only to be told that it was all a mistake and that I had better go back! I demanded to see the ADMS, the DADMS, whoever was in charge. To my delight I found that the ADMS of this composite division was none other than Colonel MacEwen, the man who had recruited me to parachuting three years earlier, and even better, the DADMS, who controlled everything medical within the division was Bobby Marquis, who had been a fellow medical student and a good friend in Edinburgh and who had joined the army and the parachutists at the same time as me. He was delighted to see me and at once agreed that I was not to go back but to stay with the division; 'Though where we shall put you, David, old boy,' he said, 'I'm damned if I know!'

PALESTINE 1946

My eight months in Palestine – March to October 1946 – were a rich period for me. Although I was increasingly uncomfortable as our army became an anti-Jewish army of occupation and repression and I felt steadily more estranged from the attitudes of the British army officers amongst whom I had to live, I had many good experiences. I no longer took my role and rank in the army seriously; I was just a civilian awaiting demobilisation, so I was able to use army skills to get myself a pleasant life.

I managed to get around extensively to visit the fascinating Middle East – to Egypt, to Cairo, the Pyramids and the Sphinx, to Athens, to see the Acropolis and the Parthenon, to Lebanon, to Beirut and Baalbeck. I toured intriguing Palestine, full of its Biblical overtones and modern challenges and above all Jerusalem, that fascinating tangle of mighty (and shabby) religious shrines.

It was a strange world in which I found myself. The war had been over for six months, and the shrinking and reorganisation of the British army was going ahead rapidly. The remnants of two airborne divisions (1st and 6th) had been combined into one; battalions and units had been fused. The new division had then been sent from England to the Middle East as a garrison force. They were stationed all over Palestine and were trying to get themselves organised. Most of those who had served since 1939 had been demobilised. Some officers and men had decided to stay in the army and had committed themselves to regular enlistment; they were keen to get things organised and working well. Many young men who had missed the war had been called up under national service; they knew they had to serve two years, and some, wishing for excitement, had volunteered for parachuting. This 'new intake' included a number of doctors. They were keen to explore the world, experience army life and have an adventure. Amongst all this keenness were people like me, civilians at heart, trapped until demobilisation, longing to get out of military life and determined to avoid danger, exertion or keenness in their remaining months in the army.

Those who were trying to hold these shrinking units together were desperate for experienced officers and Bobby Marquis tried to persuade me to stay. 'Sign on for a further six months, David, old boy! Macewen would love to have you and he would make it well worth your while. He'd make you a major and put you in charge of a field ambulance. You'd get lots of extra pay which would help when you are demobbed. I've signed on and look at me – a major, an MBE and the challenge of running the medical services, a whole division. What a wonderful opportunity!' Bobby's enthusiasm, always infectious, almost captured me but then I realised that I was sick of the army; I wanted to get out, get home, get married, start working at real doctoring again. I thanked him graciously and refused.

Sadly Bobby accepted that he could not recruit me for continuing service and sought a place for me in the division. All the field ambulances and battalions were full – but there were some gunners in an isolated camp who needed a doctor. So I was sent there in early March.

It was a dreary place, a tented camp on a bleak hillside, currently lashed by the spring rains. There was very little for me to do. Each morning I held a sick parade but could do all that was necessary in half an hour. My medical corporal, like myself, was sullenly awaiting his demob. The gunner officers were a pleasant group of young men, mostly recently enlisted, but I found no one congenial among them. They spent most evenings playing poker and drinking in the draughty tent that served as the officers mess. After a week or so of drinking too much every night to fight off boredom I faced myself and asked what I was going to do with my remaining months in the army.

I felt that my mind had deteriorated and that I was possibly no longer capable of serious intellectual work; perhaps service in the tropics had rotted my brain, perhaps years in the army had dulled any intellectual capacity that I had had. I had not studied a book since the autumn of 1942 when I worked for my finals. I had, of course, since then read books for pleasure and army manuals of instruction, but I had not studied – attempted to learn anything – for four years. Perhaps it was too late. What was I to do?

I decided to take myself in hand. I started to exercise my body, fat and flabby after months of travelling and went on cross country runs around the camp. I started to exercise my mind. I got hold of a table, a chair and a lamp and set them up in my tent. I got out my typewriter and began to spend the evenings trying to write the tale of my adventures instead of drinking dully in the mess. I bought a heavy book on contemporary European history and forced myself to study it systematically. I decided to try to learn Russian (to deal with the postwar world) and found myself a tutor, an engaging Russian lady, in Tel Aviv.

I began to explore the strange land that I was in, about which I knew little beyond compulsory Bible study at school and T.E. Lawrence's *Seven Pillars of Wisdom*. Whenever possible I took trips to the towns and cities. The first was Jerusalem, an amazing ancient city. I toured the great sites. I went round the church of the Holy Sepulchre, a dirty dilapidated ancient building, held up by 'temporary' baulks of timber, and was given a 'certificate of pilgrimage' by a smelly old man with a long beard who was a dignitary of the Greek Orthodox church. I went to the Dome of the Rock, Al Haram as Sharif, the green gleaming mosque on the ancient temple site and was shown where the Archangel Gabriel held down the rock when Mahommet leapt up to heaven. I saw the Wailing Wall, a squalid little alley where strange old men in black coats and fur rimmed hats rocked to and fro muttering watched over by a khaki clad policeman with a submachine gun. These shabby places reinforced my agnosticism and anticlericalism. I went on an organised trip to a Kibbutz and was charmed by the neat orchards and farm lands, the tough cheerful men and women in their brief shorts and the nursery full of chubby infants. This looked like a desirable and admirable future; this was socialism in action! I went into Tel Aviv and found bookshops – real bookshops, full of books that I wanted to read – the first that I had seen since leaving England nearly a year ago. I found congenial intellectuals, like the proprietor of a bookshop in Tel Aviv. I was propped up against the bookstack in his shop, busy reading, when a voice said, 'Why don't you sit down?', not sarcastic but welcoming. I sat and we chatted for an hour; he told of his boyhood in Manchester and I told of my travels in the east. At last I was back amongst civilised people.

By now I was getting mail regularly from England and was beginning to think actively about what I would do when I got home. I wrote to my professors saying that I would be home soon and would like to work with them again. But I wondered whether I could do some medicine in Palestine. Then, at a party at divisional headquarters, I met Bob Blair, the airborne division Psychiatrist, whom I had known in Bulford in my first year in the airborne and whom I had last seen on the airstrip at Pakanbaroe. He asked what I was doing and I told him of my dissatisfaction and idleness. He said that he was working on the psychiatric ward in the army hospital at Sarafand and that they needed another doctor; would I like to join them? I was delighted at a chance of medical employment; next morning we went to Bobby Marquis. He said he could spare me from divisional work for a time, and I was seconded to the 12th British general hospital, Sarafand. I moved into the hospital, into a comfortable room and reported for work at the psychiatric ward.

Then began one of the most rewarding periods of my army service. I found the ward a good place to work, my colleagues congenial, the patients interesting and the subject itself, psychiatry, fascinating. I worked, I talked with the patients, I learned from my colleagues and I studied text books. It was there that I began my lifelong study and practice of psychiatry. It was there, too, that I began to find again my identity as a doctor and that I chose the specialty that would occupy the rest of my professional life.

The hospital was housed in temporary buildings in the middle of the hot dry Palestine plain, and served the allied armies of the middle east. The psychiatric wing was small, 40 beds, on a little hill on the edge of the hospital grounds. We received mentally disturbed patients from allied army units all over the area – Palestine, Syria, Iraq, Lebanon and Cyprus and we regularly despatched

120

'boarded' men back to England. We also tried to provide referral and outpatient services for units in Palestine – particularly the airborne division.

The staff were few but able. There were three psychiatrists, all Majors; Bob Blair, the former airborne corps psychiatrist, one of the very few psychiatrists who was a trained parachutist, a bluff cheerful figure; John McCombe, a small, dour, taciturn, grey haired Scotsman, and in charge, Tony Manugian, an Armenian from Beirut. After qualifying in Beirut he had studied psychiatry at Edinburgh with my teacher, D.K. Henderson, and then gone back as deputy superintendent to the famous Asfuriyeh psychiatric hospital in Beirut. He had a great deal of affection for Britain and had volunteered for the British army at the start of the war and served throughout the war in the RAMC in the Middle East. All three had been in the army for years and had worked in mental hospitals before the war. They knew the army and they knew psychiatry and I think were rather bored with both. The arrival of someone new and eager to learn may have been quite a relief for them; at any rate they spent many hours teaching me the trade.

There were two nursing sisters and a number of RAMC nursing orderlies, some of whom had been mental nurses in asylums before being called up into the army. It was, however, from the patients that I learned most. Most were Englishmen who had broken under the strains of being conscripted soldiers sent to serve in a hostile, strange and uncomfortable land. They were depressed, demoralised, anxious, ineffective and longing to go home. Since we sympathised and identified with them, we found it only too easy to 'board' them as unfit for future army service and to despatch them home. They did not stay long with us. Every Thursday we put a draft of them into the hospital train bound for Egypt.

But it was the other patients who provided me with some of the most memorable experiences. During the war many strange people had been recruited in the British armies; now they were trying to get out, but often no one wanted them; sometimes the countries they had come from had disappeared. Worse, some of them had become mad and had landed up in Sarafand. Although few countries wanted refugees, none wanted mad refugees, so they stayed indefinitely. There was a hypomanic Armenian capering about and chattering, demanding to be sent to Soviet Armenia. There were sad paranoid Poles who felt they had nowhere to go, especially not Russian occupied Poland. There were schizophrenic Arabs and depressed Jews from the Palestine regiment, wondering what 'peace' would hold for them. There was a white Russian from Shanghai who objected to being in the Palestine regiment – he said that he was a Christian stranded in a unit for Jews and that they treated him unfairly. There were Maltese criminals who had landed in the British army military prison and having faked insanity, had landed in Sarafand. There were even a few women, locally recruited army auxiliaries.

My attempts to talk with these people, to understand their suffering and their symptoms, to grasp the strange life paths that had brought them to this desolate place were fascinating. With many it was fairly easy; demoralised Englishmen talked of the dullness and brutality of life in isolated army units with nothing to do and how their depression and anxiety had gradually unmanned them until they had been forced to the ignominious expedient of seeing a 'trick cyclist', being labelled as 'bonkers' and 'boarded out on a one-way ticket to Blighty'. But others were more complex. I remember a black private from an east African regiment who was brought in in a withdrawn catatonic state; he lay on the floor, groaning. To attempt to communicate with him I had two interpreters – a corporal from his unit who could speak the man's tribal language and translate it into Swahili and another to interpret Swahili into English. I did not learn much about the unfortunate man who was later sent back to east Africa, still catatonic. I recall another Indian corporal chattering in agitated distress. I asked the interpreter what the man was saying, only to be told, 'Oh, this is a very bad man, Captain Sahib. He is truly bad. I say to him, why do you not stand up and salute when the Captain Sahib speaks to you – and all he will tell me is monkey talk and bad words. I do not think you can help this bad man, Sahib'. He was right; there was little I could do to help him. However, he settled down and went back to his unit.

I saw the classic psychoses – acute schizophrenia, raging catatonia and florid hallucinosis; hypomanic and even raging mania, the classic Bell's mania. I saw depression and anxiety in many forms, even including classic conversion hysteria. We treated them with the best treatments available in those days. Tranquillisers had not been invented; the sedatives were chloral and paraldehyde and opiates; the only effective control of mania was by dangerous doses of the barbiturates. I was interested to see the new treatment electroplexy (ECT) which had come into use since my student days. I saw men plunged in deep immovable depressive misery and even stupor amazingly relieved by a few treatments. We used pentothal narcosis (narcoanalysis) considerably; I remember one very dramatic cure of blindness due to hysteria.

So I went through all the excitement of the early days of learning psychiatry, seeing cures and heartening recoveries. I studied what textbooks I could find, buy in Tel Aviv, or borrow, especially that delightful volume Curran and Guttmann's *Psychological Medicine* (the first early slim edition) which presented a fresh and witty look at the psychiatric problems presented to a young services doctor. I began to know the trade and determined to train properly as a psychiatrist once I got home.

I even began to get some inklings of what would later become social psychiatry and rehabilitation. I watched the rise and fall of depression (i.e. morale) in the unit as the results of medical boards came through. I saw the potent effect of our occupational therapist – 'the countess'. She was a Russian painter from Jerusalem, a talented artist of about 60. She ran painting classes and the depressed demoralised English working class men especially benefited. These men had left school at 14 to go into dead-end jobs and then the army; they had never painted in their lives. Now they were daubing vigorously and the countess was telling them they had artistic talent and sensibility. The combination of creative activity, warm hearted Russian praise and the knowledge that they were going home was far more effective for them than ECT. Their depressions lifted, their anxiety settled, their sleep improved. Their departure was often highly dramatic, for the countess always came to see them off; as she told me one Thursday, 'Thees morning I am so 'appy and so sad; so 'appy because my boys are going 'ome – so sad because they are leaving me. I cry, they cry, we all cry together. It was wonderful'.

I managed one good trip while at the hospital. Major Manugian was demobilized and was going back to his home in Beirut. I went up with him and spent four days in Lebanon, just before the last British troops left and the country became independent. In Beirut I met again my guide from Damascus; he took me round the shops and the souks and arranged visits for me to the last Cedars of Lebanon, high in the mountains, and to the mighty temple of Jupiter at Baalbeck – once one of the seven wonders of the world.

On the way back I had an experience which has remained with me as a measure of the antiquity of the Levant. The jeep I was in stopped briefly where a ridge and a river pressed the road against the coast. Looking idly around, I saw an inscription recording that this bridge Nasr-el-Kelb had been liberated in 1941 by the free French forces; then I noticed another plaque with a rising sun celebrating its liberation in 1917 by the Australian ANZAC Corps; than another dated 1801 celebrating its capture by Napoleon Bonaparte. Then I searched further and found inscriptions in Egyptian hieroglyphics and in Assyrian cuneiform. Every army for 4,000 years had had to fight to capture this spot – and had to celebrate their success. The only ones who had refrained were the Muslims who did not believe in boasting!

While I had been settling in to work in the hospital, things were changing in Palestine. I knew that there had been trouble in Palestine ever since Allenby conquered it from the Turks during World War I. 'Troubles' in the British protectorate had often been in the newspapers in the thirties. I knew too that the Jews who had helped the allied war effort against Germany in World War I had been granted a 'national home' in Palestine in 1917 and that they had begun to make the barren land fertile. In the thirties the Arabs had started rioting and attacking the British and the Jews. Their leader the 'Mufti of Jerusalem' had agitated against us before the war and then had become an ally of Hitler. Many Palestine Jews had joined the British army in the Palestine regiment and had fought well in Italy. I had expected that after the war, Britain would again support the Jews in their attempt to build up the national home in Palestine, particularly since the Nazis, our enemies, had treated them so badly. When I first came into Palestine in February 1946 I found great friendliness from Jewish people and goodwill to us, the paratroopers who had smashed Nazism.

Gradually it began to emerge that things would not be so simple. It seemed that the new British government and especially the powerful foreign secretary, Ernest Bevin, were hostile to the Jews. It seemed that the Jews had found many Jewish refugees from extermination camps in Europe and that they wanted to bring them all to Palestine, but the British government would not let them, and we, the British troops on the spot, were to be used to prevent them. There were stories of attempted landings, of arrests and of scuffles. Then the British government set up internment camps in Cyprus and put the people from the boats into them. We were putting in prison the very people whom we had liberated from Nazi extermination camps!

Then the British authorities started ordering searches of Jewish settlements for illicit arms, and used the parachute battalions to do this work. Our soldiers searched the houses in the destructive style that they had learned in occupied Europe and looted as they had done there. Jewish protests and hostility rose, and the *'Kaladiots'* (poppies), as the Red Berets were called, became unpopular. I was no longer welcome in Tel Aviv with my red beret. We were warned not to go out alone and to wear guns whenever we went outside camp. Guards were placed on the gates of camps and sentries became vigilant. It appeared that both Jews and Arabs wanted any guns they could get and were offering high prices in the bazaars. There were raids on armouries, at first cheekily successful, but then bloody and fatal. Members of raiding parties who were caught were tried, sentenced to death and executed. The atmosphere got steadily nastier.

It was clear that in due course there would be an open struggle between the Jews and the Arabs in Palestine; the British soldiers seemed to be cast as reluctant and ineffective referees. I personally had no doubt where my sympathies lay. I had seen the Kibbutzim, the towns and cities and green farms and orchards that the Jews had created and had met them, charming, intelligent, cultured Europeans. I had seen the Palestine Arabs, squalid peasants, and had seen how they beat their animals and had heard that they treated their black garbed women no better. I knew they had hoped that our enemies, the Nazis, would win the war. I saw little to admire or like in them. I was, as one colleague put it, 'For the settlers and against the Indians'.

All this did not affect my personal life within the hospital very much. We seldom went out; even going for a swim meant a convoy, armed guards and loaded side arms. But I was busy and happy with my professional work. But what distressed me deeply was what I heard in the officers' messes, even in the hospital doctors' mess. Often during my army life I had heard fascist and antisemitic remarks by some of the more stupid and reactionary of the officers, especially regulars, but they were usually muttered asides. Now they were strident and outspoken. 'Just what you'd expected of the bloody Yids, biting the hand that fed them?', 'What do they think they're doing – we saved their bloody lives, didn't we?' – and even more sinister – 'You know I reckon old Hitler was right about one thing; we should have let him get on with it and wipe out all the Yids. Now we're going to have to finish the job off for him!' I was appalled and furious. Was this what I had fought for, to allow these swine to raise their heads again? I was angry and impotent, and also ashamed that I did not speak up. Some of the other doctors felt as I did and we would have drinking sessions in our rooms deploring the things colleagues said. But we seldom spoke up openly.

It was a sickening and bitter time for me. I was a member of an army of occupation that was persecuting the people I admired and had worked with. Fortunately I was never put to the test; I was never ordered to take part in the search missions carried out by the parachutists, I was never asked to do anything wicked or illegal or unprofessional. On the ward we treated Jewish and Arab patients alike. But I hated the position I was in, deplored the orders of the Palestine command and hated Bevin for having put us, the proud parachutists, to do his dirty political work. I felt that I was being forced to be ashamed of the beret I had worn with such pride.

I had four good months working in the hospital but at the end of July I was called back to divisional work. However, I could hardly complain; I knew that my demob was very near and I was given a job that was the envy of the other doctors. I was 'Medical Officer to the Parachute Training School' at RAF Acquir. This meant living in the comfort of an RAF officers mess with nothing to do, for

126

parachute training had been suspended! My only job was to examine volunteers for parachuting to see if they were fit – an easy routine job. But it led to the most fascinating of all my Middle East trips, during August 1946; I was sent off with two other officers to examine parachute volunteers in other commands.

We went down to Cairo. We travelled down by jeep, across the famous Sinai desert. We stopped in Beersheba, a dusty little market town, where I saw my first real Bedouin, a tall, handsome, hawk-nosed, black-bearded man, arrogant in flowing white clothes, so different from the grubby cringing brown Palestinian peasants. We spent a week in Cairo; I visited the Pyramids, climbing to the top of the Great Pyramid of Cheops; I went to the Cairo museum and I saw the staggering gold of Tutankhamun.

We were sent to Greece, to Athens and Salonika. A civil war was going on and there was sporadic firing in the streets; the ancient sites were entirely deserted. I walked the Acropolis all on my own and wondered at the Parthenon and the delicately pink columns against the vivid blue sky. I visited the spring of Aesculapius below the Acropolis and renewed my dedication to medicine. The trip to Athens was a revelation to me. All my life I had been hearing about the ancient Greeks and discussing them as an odd obsession of our teachers of classics. Suddenly I realised what an amazing people they had been and how they had laid the foundations of our culture.

I came back to RAF Acquir and then my demobilisation group's date was announced. I wrote home and told the family; Mary Rose wrote of the arrangements she was making for our wedding and honeymoon. I began to pack my bags and say farewell to my patients. The day arrived and I got on the 'demob express' that ran south through the derelict Arab lands of south Palestine to Gaza and then through the desert to the Canal, into Egypt and on to Alexandria, a pleasing city by the sea. We travelled across the Mediterranean in a small troopship and landed in southern France. Then through France by train, across the Channel and straight to the demobilisation centre. I was issued with a civilian suit, shoes, raincoat and an absurd little hat and I was out of the army.

All arrangements had been made by Mary Rose and our wedding took place a few days later. For the last time I donned my best uniform, with wings, medals and treasured red beret. Amidst family good wishes we set off for a honeymoon in Switzerland.

After two delightful weeks in a peaceful undamaged land we returned to Edinburgh, to the coldest winter for 50 years, the austerities of postwar British life and the toil of postgraduate medical studies.